M000308013

The Wrath of God

Rev. Livio Fanzaga

The Wrath of God
How to Read the Signs of the Times and Recognize the Evils of Our Age

Translated by A. J. O'Brien

SOPHIA INSTITUTE PRESS
Manchester, New Hampshire

Copyright ©1997 by Sugarco Edizioni S.t.l., Milan, Italy

English translation Copyright © 2022 by Sophia Institute Press

The Wrath of God was originally published as *Wrath of God: The Days of the Antichrist* by Roman Catholic Books, Fort Collins, Colorado, in 1998.

Printed in the United States of America. All rights reserved.

Cover design by LUCAS Art & Design, Jenison, MI.

On the cover: The Expulsion from Paradise (1740), by Charles Joseph Natoire (HRJH16) © Science History Images / Alamy Stock Photo.

Unless otherwise noted, Scripture quotations are taken from the Jerusalem Bible, Copyright © 1966, 1967, 1968 by Darton, Longmand & Todd LTD and Doubleday and Co. Inc. All rights reserved.

No part of this book may be reproduced, stored in a retrieval system, or transmitted in any form, or by any means, electronic, mechanical, photocopying, or otherwise, without the prior written permission of the publisher, except by a reviewer, who may quote brief passages in a review.

Sophia Institute Press

Box 5284, Manchester, NH 03108

1-800-888-9344

www.SophiaInstitute.com

Sophia Institute Press is a registered trademark of Sophia Institute.

paperback ISBN 978-1-64413-608-9

ebook ISBN 978-1-64413-609-6

Library of Congress Control Number: 2022930398

First printing

Contents

Note to the 1998 Edition

This book consists of the transcripts of two broadcasts,[1] made on Radio Maria, by Fr. Livio Fanzaga in 1993 and 1994. To these has been added a final section which develops and synthesizes the main themes of the first two sections. Some adaptation was necessary in the transposition from oral to written form. The book is a commentary on two texts with a common subject, written nearly a century ago. Both explore the manifestation of the Antichrist at the end of the world. This is an important theme in the context of Christian proclamation, for it has never ceased to evoke lively pastoral and doctrinal interest in the Church. While it is sometimes neglected in contemporary preaching, nevertheless, for many of the faithful it remains an object of particular fascination, prayer, curiosity, and fear.

The object of this book is not simply to illustrate the end of the world and the appearance of the Antichrist by reading two

---

[1] The broadcasts were accompanied by excerpts from various composers, which provide a form of musical commentary to accompany the subject matter. These included "Dies irae" in Gregorian chant; "Kyrie" from Joseph Haydn's *Missa in Angustiis*; "Te Deum" of Joseph Haydn; "Dies irae" of Giuseppe Verdi; and "Recordare Jesu Pie" from Luigi Perosi's *Giudizio Universale*.

gripping books, one by the Russian author Vladimir Soloviev, the other by an English Catholic, Robert Hugh Benson. Apart from the delight of discovering two absorbing works of literature, the reader will have an opportunity to revisit and contemplate the Old and New Testaments and their descriptions of the eschatological conflict between God and his enemies. Fr. Livio will explain and comment on these mysterious and difficult passages, in the light of the interpretation which the Church ascribes to them, especially in the *Catechism of the Catholic Church*.

This doctrinal framework will afford criteria by which to evaluate the literary works in question and some more recent publications on the same subject. These latter, usually concerned with the end of the world and the coming of the Antichrist, abound. Hence our interest in this subject is motivated by its fantastic aspects and less so by its picturesque side which is often accompanied by various kinds of speculation about the end of the world as it tries to interpret what is an authentic aspect of the Christian faith.

Author Livio evaluates concerns drawn from two books which are well beyond the level of the merely curious and ephemeral — which seeks to know the *how* and the *when* of the world's end. He highlights the extent to which both texts understand and grasp the meaning and intention of Sacred Scripture by a genuine and proper exegesis. Secondly, and perhaps the most important aspect of this book, he underlines in a passionate way the contemporary relevance of Soloviev and Benson. Aside from the amusing or naive particular details of the narratives and their chronological order, both writers display an extraordinary capacity to intuit the impending end from the signs of the times in which they lived. Both believed the end of the world to be close to hand. Both saw the seeds of the final conflict between God and his Adversary. They predicted the end of the world would come in our own time.

Padre Livio asks which of the signs of their times are to be seen in our world. Which of Benson's and Soloviev's seeds have reached maturity in today's world and in the contemporary Church? Just how prophetic are Benson and Soloviev, these vigilant and believing Christians?

Another equally disquieting question must follow this last one: Have we come to the end of the world?

Fr. Livio's response to these questions will fill our hearts with peace, because in encountering Christ, the meaning of our personal existence as well as of history is revealed.

The book's title has been altered slightly for English-language readers.

Dies irae

Dies irae, dies illa
solvet saeclum in favilla
teste David cum Sibylla.

Quantus tremor est futurus
quando judex est venturus
cuncta stricte discussurus!

Tuba, mirum spargens sonum
per sepulcra regionum,
coget omnes ante thronum.

Mors stupebit et natura,
cum resurget creatura,
judicanti responsura.

Liber scriptus proferetur,
in quo totum continetur,
unde mundus judicetur.

Judex ergo cum sedebit,
quidquid latet apparebit,
nil inultum remanebit.

The Wrath of God

Quid sum, miser, tunc dicturus,
quem patronum rogaturus,
cum vix justus sit securus?

Rex tremendae majestatis,
qui salvandos salvas gratis,
salva me, fons pietatis!

Recordare, Jesu pie,
quod sum causa tuae viae:
ne me perdas illa die.

Quaerens me sedisti lassus,
redemisti Crucem passus:
tantus labor non sit cassus.

Juste judex ultionis,
donum fac remissionis
ante diem rationis.

Ingemisco tamquam reus:
culpa rubet vultus meus:
supplicanti parce, Deus.

Qui Mariam absolvisti
et latronem exaudisti,
mihi quoque spem dedisti.

Preces meae non sunt dignae,
sed tu bonus fac benigne,
ne perenni cremer igne.

Inter oves locum praesta
et ab haedis me sequestra,
statuens in parte dextra.

Confutatis maledictis,
flammis acribus addictis,
voca me cum benedictis.

Oro supplex et acclinis
cor contritum quasi cinis,
gere curam mei finis.

Lacrimosa dies illa
qua resurget ex favilla
judicandus homo reus.
Huic ergo parce, Deus.

Pie Iesu Domine,
dona eos requie.[2]

Amen.

---

[2] The form *dona eos requie* is grammatically correct, as is that used in
the liturgy for the sequence, *dona eis requiem*, but to be preferred
for metrical reasons.

Day of Wrath

Day of wrath and doom impending,
David's word with Sibyl's blending!
Heaven and earth in ashes ending!

O, what fear man's bosom rendeth,
When from heaven the Judge descendeth,
On whose sentence all dependeth!

Wondrous sound the trumpet flingeth,
Through earth's sepulchers it ringeth,
All before the throne it bringeth.

Death is struck, and nature quaking,
All creation is awaking,
To its Judge an answer making.

Lo! the book exactly worded,
Wherein all hath been recorded;
Thence shall judgment be awarded.

When the Judge His seat attaineth,
And each hidden deed arraigneth,
Nothing unavenged remaineth.

The Wrath of God

What shall I, frail man, be pleading?
Who for me be interceding,
When the just are mercy needing?

King of majesty tremendous,
Who dost free salvation send us,
Fount of pity, then befriend us!

Think, kind Jesu! my salvation
Caused Thy wondrous Incarnation;
Leave me not to reprobation.

Faint and weary Thou hast sought me,
On the Cross of suffering bought me;
Shall such grace be vainly brought me?

Righteous Judge! for sin's pollution
Grant Thy gift of absolution,
Ere that day of retribution.

Guilty, now I pour my moaning,
All my shame with anguish owning;
Spare, O God, Thy suppliant groaning!

Through the sinful woman shriven,
Through the dying thief forgiven,
Thou to me a hope hast given.

Worthless are my prayers and sighing,
Yet, good Lord, in grace complying,
Rescue me from fires undying.

With Thy favored sheep O place me,
Nor among the goats abase me,
But to Thy tight hand upraise me.

While the wicked are confounded,
Doomed to flames of woe unbounded,
Call me with Thy saints surrounded.

Low I kneel, with heart-submission,
Crushed to ashes in contrition;
Help me in my last condition!

Ah! that day of tears and mourning!
From the dust of earth returning,
Man for judgment must prepare him;
Spare, O God, in mercy spare him!

Lord all-pitying, Jesu Blest,
Grant them Thine eternal rest.[3]

---

[3] Matthew Britt, *The Hymns of the Breviary and Missal* (New York, 1922), gives this translation of the Dies Irae of Dr. W. J. Irons.

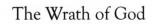

The Wrath of God

Introduction

My aim is to present and explore with you the theme of the Antichrist. It is a complex but interesting subject which, during the course of history, has lent itself to many interpretations. In our own times, for various reasons, this subject has acquired a renewed vitality.

The proclamation of the end of the world is part of the teaching of Jesus. It was one of the most important themes in primitive Christianity and remains a subject of permanent interest for the Church.

Contemporary preaching, however, is for the most part silent on this subject, so much so that today the theme of the Antichrist has been appropriated almost exclusively by the sects. Their preaching commands lively attention. The end of the world is often at its very heart. Perhaps such interest is born of something like a feeling of uncertainty that is peculiar to these closing years of the millennium.[4]

While the end of the world and the appearance of the Antichrist is often overlooked by the preaching of the Church, it has

---

[4] Recall that this book was first published in 1997; hence the author's references to the end of the millennium. — Ed.

become the object of numerous private "messages" imparted in presumed private revelations.

This book does not intend further to multiply such messages. The impetus to revisit this subject came to me following an address by Cardinal Giacomo Biffi to a meeting of Communion and Liberation (CL) at Rimini in 1992. He broached the subject of the Antichrist by quoting the great Russian writer, Soloviev. The text from the *Tale* quoted by the Cardinal encouraged me to reread Soloviev. Pleasing and captivating, the *Tale* was ideal for a radio broadcast where it could be read and commented on.

In a subsequent interview, Cardinal Biffi emphasized the prophetic admonishment of Soloviev's *Tale*. What kind of Antichrist does Soloviev portray?

According to Cardinal Biffi, quoting Soloviev, the Antichrist was

> "a convinced idealist. He believed in the Good, even in God, but he only loved himself. The inordinate pride of the great idealist seemed justified both by his exceptional genius, beauty and nobility, and his lofty asceticism, disinterestedness and active philanthropy. From his earliest youth he was marked out as a learned and incisive exegete."

Soloviev's description of the Antichrist as a pacifist, an ecologist, and an ecumenist deserves further reflection.

> At the beginning he has no hostility against Jesus. He recognized His good intentions and His lofty teaching. Three things about Jesus were unacceptable to him: firstly, His moral preoccupations; then His claim to uniqueness; and the third thing the Antichrist could not accept about Christ was that He lives, so much so that he screams to himself repeatedly: "He is not living, He is not and shall not be. He rotted in the tomb, rotted like the lowest ...!"

The times will come, said Soloviev, indeed we could say that they are already here, when within Christianity—which cannot be embraced except by a courageous act of faith—there will be a tendency to dissolve the fact of salvation into commodities to be sold on a worldly market. Hence Christianity is reduced to humanitarian activities, social work, solidarity, philanthropy, and culture. The Christian message is identified with a commitment to dialogue between nations and religions, to the pursuit of well-being and progress, and exhortations to respect nature. These are all good things in themselves but they are *consequences* of belief in Christ. They cannot, however, be *identified* with the core of Christianity. The Church is that of the living God, as St. Paul says, and is the pillar of truth and its foundation. Exchanging it for a cultural, beneficent, or social organization would be mortally insidious; but this is what is happening today among those who have been redeemed by the precious Blood of Christ.

Jesus Christ, the Crucified and Risen Son of God, man's only Savior, cannot be traded for some well-intentioned projects or motivations which belong to the mundane mentality which prevails today. Jesus Christ is a rock, as He said Himself. On this rock we shall build by trusting in Him—otherwise we are lost. In Christ, who is the fullness of the Father, man is fulfilled and discovers his only hope.

Some Questions

This was Cardinal Biffi's presentation of the Antichrist.

However, we would like to know a little more. Clearly, Soloviev's description is not exhaustive nor, indeed, is that of other writers, however good they may be.

Is this portrait of the Antichrist merely a literary fiction or is it solidly based on Scripture?

In the light of the Bible, what are the basic features of the Antichrist? To what extent is the time of the Antichrist constitutive of the Christian vision of history? What does the doctrine of the Church teach about the Antichrist?

Here we shall make a brief outline of the biblical texts referring to the Antichrist and present those sections of the *Catechism of the Catholic Church* which address this subject. Then we shall read the text of Soloviev's *Tale* and comment upon it. Following that, we shall examine another writer's work exploring the same theme, R. H. Benson's *Lord of the World*.

Both texts are extraordinarily relevant. But they must be assessed and measured by the yard stick of Scripture and the authoritative teaching of the Church. While Benson and Soloviev are great writers, perhaps even prophetic writers, the Bible is the Word of God and the Magisterium of the Church is its authentic interpretation. We must have recourse to these sources if we desire to know how the Word of God describes the Antichrist and if we are to have a sure guide for our study of these two books.

Biblical Texts concerning the Antichrist

To avoid all charges of subjectivism, I wish to turn to Léon-Dufour's *Dictionary of Biblical Theology*. From the point of view of conformity to the Church's Magisterium it is extremely useful. The article which it contains on the Antichrist was written by two famous exegetes: Béda Rigaux and Pierre Grelot.

The term "Antichrist" denotes one who sets himself against Christ. It occurs exclusively in three places in letters of St. John: 1 John 2:18-22; 4:3; and 2 John 7. While these are the only texts to use the term, the reality which it denotes is present in many of the apocalyptic texts of the New Testament: Mark 13:14ff, 2 Thessalonians 2:3–12, and Revelation 13:4–18, the famous passage of the two beasts.

These passages were not written in a vacuum. They belong to a context which has a dualistic vision of history, already present in the Old Testament, which prefigures the Antichrist albeit in an imprecise manner. From its very opening pages, the Bible portrays the figure of the one who opposes God's plan, God's adversary par excellence, Satan. The action of God operates against this opposing force which, at different times in history, assumes different forms. Human history contains many forces strongly opposed to God: Satan uses this nation at one time, or this person at another, to thwart God's saving plan for this world.

In the drama of the first temptation and fall of Adam and Eve (Gen. 3), the serpent, representing Satan, vents his hostility to God. Satan continues to oppose God and the servants of God within human history by manipulating human forces. According to the Bible, the enemies of God's people are enemies of God himself, because through them the Adversary par excellence sets himself against the designs of God's Providence. This was true of Egypt at the time of the Exodus, and of the empires of Assur and Babylon which adored false gods and oppressed the people of Israel in their attempt to exercise spiritual dominion over Israel. The same is true of those pagan kings who desired to be worshipped as divinities. These incarnate Satan's opposition to God in historical forces.

This is an unceasing history which continues until the final conflict which Ezekiel (38–39) regards as the definitive defeat of Gog, king of Magog. The final triumph of Yahweh will inaugurate the era of eschatological salvation.

In the Old Testament the person who most incarnates Satan's opposition to God is Antiochus Epiphanes, in the book of Daniel.

He is the enemy of Israel and persecutor of the true worshippers of God. Daniel portrays this oppressor as the impious one who tries to take the place of God (see 11:36) and as the impious one who profanes the holy place with the abomination of desolation (9:27; 11:31; 12:11). He tries to deceive the people into rejecting God and worshiping the false idols of paganism. In 2 Thessalonians, Paul takes up the legacy of Daniel to describe the Antichrist. Daniel (7:8) says that he is the eleventh horn on the fourth head of the beast with the satanic face. The defeat of Antiochus Epiphanes, who incarnates historical opposition to God, begins the era of God's Kingdom (see 12:1). From the Old Testament on, the message is clear: God alone reigns and Satan, who machinates against His plans through various historical manifestations, will be defeated as well as those who consort with him.

The New Testament authors Matthew, Mark, John, and Paul take up the Old Testament perspective and clarify it. The Anti-God of the Old Testament, the adversary of God, becomes the Antichrist of the New Testament.

Christ's adversary is already at work through his followers. In the New Testament, he who opposes Christ operates through concrete historical forces. He is manifest from the first moment of Christ's presence and will continue with his opposition until the eschatological duel, at the end of time. Then he will be definitively defeated.

While the word "Antichrist" is used only in St. John's letters, the teaching on the Antichrist is clearly present in the Gospels, in the letters of St. Paul, and in the book of Revelation.

Having reviewed the New Testament texts, we can say that the Bible illustrates a clear and well-structured line of thought on the Antichrist. Let us examine these texts in historical sequence from the first preaching: the preaching of Jesus contained in the

Gospels, in Paul's letter to the Thessalonians, which was probably written before the Gospels, and finally, in Revelation and the letters of St. John.

In the Gospels, the "apocalyptic synopsis" — the vision of the period between the first and second coming of Christ (Matt. 24; Mark 13; Luke 21:5-33) — Jesus proclaims the great tribulation that is a prelude to the glorious coming of the Son of Man. False Christs (Mark 13:22) will arise during this tribulation. Their seduction will bring many to apostasy. His sign will be the abomination of desolation (Mark 13:14) placed in the holy sanctuary (Matt. 24:15). This means that apostasy will happen in the Church. It will detach Christians from the worship of Christ and turn them to the worship of the man of iniquity, as Paul calls it in 2 Thessalonians 2:3.

In the eschatological discourse, as recounted by Mark (13:5-10), Jesus speaks of the great trial, tribulation, and the need for perseverance until the end of time:

> Take care that no one deceives you. Many will come using my name and saying, "I am he," and they will deceive many. When you hear of wars and rumors of wars, do not be alarmed, this is something that must happen, but the end will not be yet. For nation will fight against nation, and kingdom against kingdom. There will be earthquakes here and there; there will be famines. This is the beginning of the birth pangs. Be on your guard: they will hand you over to sanhedrins; you will be beaten in synagogues; and you will stand before governors and kings for my sake, to bear witness before them, since the Good News must first be proclaimed to all the nations.

Evidently, we are speaking of the future because we are speaking of proclaiming the Gospel to all nations. Two great trials to be sustained by the Church are prefigures: the first, persecution ("they will hand you over to sanhedrins; you will be flogged in the synagogues"), the other, perhaps more terrible, seduction. At the very heart of the Church itself, false prophets will arise and deceive many saying "I am he." (What must happen within the Church is very clearly illustrated in St. John.)

At verse 14 of the same chapter, Mark, explicitly referring to the book of Daniel, describes the seduction: "When you see *the disastrous abomination* set up where it ought not to be, (let the reader understand [Daniel]), then those in Judaea must escape to the mountains." In addition to external persecution there will also be internal apostasy. The faith will be profaned. Another faith will be proposed. Here the "disastrous abomination" will be set up where it ought not to be, inside of God's holy temple.

The synoptic accounts of the apocalypse are highly important. Christ did not abandon the themes of the Old Testament and especially that of Daniel. His preaching and that of the apostles include subjects such as the great tribulation, the great seduction, the deception of false prophets, the great persecution, and the abomination of desolation in God's holy temple. Hence, these subjects have a special authority.

The most important and explicit text concerning the Antichrist is found in St. Paul's second letter to the Thessalonians. Here Paul presents the Adversary of the end times, the being of perdition, a true Anti-God comparable to those of the Old Testament. However, he is also an Antichrist who imitates the marks of the Lord and His promise and His moment of triumph which is fixed by God. Paul emphasizes his supernatural powers and his false prodigies which are designed to bring man to ruin. *The man of iniquity*, the adversary, will complete Satan's work here on earth. He will be the paramount example of the *mystery of iniquity*, the precursor of the Evil One and of the mystery of evil which is already being deployed in the world. Many will err because of him. They cling to delusions and abandon the truth. If the man of iniquity has not already appeared it is because someone or something restrains him. Paul never explained this enigmatic allusion. It can be explained by saying that the Antichrist, the man of iniquity, whom Satan uses to attack Christ, needs to have a receptive historical context of impiety and apostasy, of a world sunken in vice and estranged from God. He also needs an introspective Church which has lost its evangelical strength and vigor.

The man of iniquity, in any event, is the prelude for the parousia of Christ who will destroy him by His coming in glory. It is absolutely necessary to read this passage:

> To turn now, brothers, to the coming of Our Lord Jesus Christ and how we shall all be gathered around him: please do not get excited too soon or alarmed by any prediction or rumor or any letter claiming to come from us, implying that the Day of the Lord has already arrived. Never let anyone deceive you in this way. (2 Thess. 2:1–3)

It would almost seem that Paul is alluding to our own times: How many claim to know when Jesus is coming!

> It cannot happen until the great revolt has taken place and the Rebel, the Lost one, has appeared. This is the Enemy, the one who claims to be so much greater than all that men call "god," that he enthrones himself in God's sanctuary and claims that he is God. (2 Thess. 2:3–4)

The Antichrist will not come as a political power nor as an ideology. He will come as a presence in the world, which will come before the end of the world. It will come before the second coming of Christ and will flourish in the context of great apostasy. It is then that Satan will play his final hand in his attempt to rid the world of Christ.

Paul calls him "man of iniquity," "son of perdition," or the son of the Evil One because he has profoundly espoused his spirit. He defines him as the one who sets himself against every object worshipped as God. His unbounded pride is characteristic of his perversity and probably the reason for his unbelief in God. He believes he is God incarnate amongst men. The Antichrist is not a delinquent or a dissolute or someone sunken in immorality (as Benson and Soloviev intuited). Rather, he is the complete contrary.

Pride characterizes his perversity. He worships himself, makes himself equal to God and sets himself up in the temple of God instead of God. He could easily be someone of great moral standing, intelligence, rectitude, and devoted to mankind to the point of believing himself to be man's savior. The characteristic pride of the Antichrist, however, is well disguised.

Paul continues: "Surely you remember me telling you about this when I was with you? And you know too, what is still holding him back from appearing before his appointed time" (2 Thess. 2:5-6). In order for him to appear, the Antichrist must have a context of great apostasy, for otherwise he would lack the fertile ground for his work and he would not be accepted.

The mystery of iniquity is already in action. Satan, the supreme Antichrist, the *man of iniquity,* is the powerful incarnation of evil, and is always at work. But that which restrains him must first be removed. For as long as the Church is strong and powerful, for as long as it is a pillar of strength, Satan cannot appear with that power with which he seeks to conquer. Only then will the impious one be revealed—only when the Church ceases to be strong.

The Lord will kill him with the breath of his mouth and will annihilate him with his glorious appearance at his coming. But when the Rebel comes, Satan will set to work: there will be all kinds of miracles and a deceptive show of signs and portents, and everything evil that can deceive those who are bound for destruction because they would not grasp the love of the truth which could have saved them. (2 Thess. 2:8-11)

The Antichrist will be supported by the powerful, the media, and he will even work miracles such as unceasing peace and Christian unity.... I mention this in reference to Soloviev's *Tale*.

This is a very important passage. Paul emphasizes that the power of the Antichrist is one of seduction—not of persecution. Christians will be persecuted at the end of the world. The Antichrist, however, will not act as a persecutor but as a seducer.

The reason why God is sending a power to delude them and make them believe what is untrue is to condemn all who refused to believe in the truth and chose wickedness instead. (2 Thess. 2:11-12)

Those who will believe the seduction of the Antichrist will not have a pure heart. Those of pure heart, the humble and the meek, like Christ, cannot be seduced by the Antichrist. Those who allow themselves to be seduced will be condemned.

This is the most famous and important passage about the Antichrist. It is also limited because Paul does not make reference to the historical forces which bear Satan's work, but only to its greatest manifestation: *the man of iniquity*. He will precede the end of the world and, it would appear, will work from within religion. He is not a persecutor but a seducer who, with every impious deception, draws people away from the truth.

The Wrath of God

The book of Revelation does not use the word Antichrist but it does speak of the historical manifestation of him who is his supreme incarnation, Satan. It evokes an apocalyptic prospect, similar to Paul's, by reference to the monstrous beasts which it describes in chapter 13. The first of these represents political power which blasphemes against God. It resembles a panther. It must be adored. It persecutes Christians — this is a component of the persecution of the end times. The second resembles a lamb with the voice of a dragon. It apes Christ, the true lamb, and performs false prodigies so that man might adore the panther. It is a powerful seducer — and thus encompasses another characteristic of the end times, seduction.

According to Xavier Léon-Dufour, the work of Satan will be accomplished here on earth by the old dragon, which transfers its evil power to the first beast, while the second, which seduces under a religious guise, will bring men to worship political power.

This is a symbolic evocation, referring obliquely to the seduction of the Church which was persecuted by the pagans of the Roman Empire. However, it also encompasses the tribulations of the end times which will be composed of the things Jesus mentions in his preaching: persecution (the first beast, standing for political power) and seduction (the second beast, representing a false religious authority).

In Brief

The first and obvious conclusion to which we have given consideration (as a modern theologian says) is that, notwithstanding the fact that in history ideas and systems have been identified with the Antichrist (because many have been crazed into identifying the Antichrist with this or that idea, this or that person, this or that political regime) and the fact that exaggerations have been made about the Antichrist, and the term has been abused, we cannot justify his elimination from Christian life and theology. It is important to stress this point. The Antichrist, as outlined here, forms part of the Christian message. It is part of our faith and belongs to the Christian vision of history.

The supreme Antichrist, Satan, he who opposes God and, following the Incarnation of the Word, opposes Christ, continues to oppose Him and will continue to do so until the end of history. All the rebellious angels have joined forces with him. Satan's opposition is made present through precise historical forces. In the Old Testament they were Egypt, Assur, Babylon, and their sovereigns. In the New Testament they can be political forces such as the Roman Empire, or heretical religious movements which deny the truth of Jesus and afflict the Church. It is thus no surprise that writers such as John should allude to the Antichrist already present in the ecclesial realities of their times.

Biblical teaching also clearly alludes to a specific incarnation of Satan, the most frightening, which, in the context of the apostasy of the end times, will unleash the final assault.

From this perspective, it is completely licit for Christians to discern from various historical movements Satan's attempts to subvert the design of God's Providence through persecution and seduction. Every era can produce historical figures, political regimes, and ideologies which incarnate Satan's opposition to Christ. We can say that every historical era has its own Antichrist.

Church Doctrine on This Subject

We have underlined that the reality of the Antichrist is a part of our faith. Following our study of the biblical texts about the Antichrist, it is useful to present the Church's doctrine about the Antichrist by referring to its most recent, authoritative, and official document:

the *Catechism of the Catholic Church*. It deals with the question of the Antichrist in articles 675, 676, and 677, in the context of the glorious return of Christ, preceded by the Church's ultimate trial.

This exercise is useful because it helps us to distinguish doctrine from interpretations or dramatizations of the Bible, such as we find in the works of Soloviev and Benson—which we shall be presenting. By stating the Church's doctrine on the Antichrist, it will be possible to evaluate these works and others like them on same subject. Article 675 of the *Catechism of the Catholic Church*, under the title "The Church's ultimate trial," states: "Before Christ's second coming the Church must pass through a final trial that will shake the faith of many believers." Thus the persecution will be a tremendous trial for the faith. "The persecution that accompanies her pilgrimage on earth will unveil the 'mystery of iniquity' in the form of a religious deception offering men an apparent solution to their problems at the price of apostasy from the truth." The Antichrist will come under the form of seduction, a religious impostor, as a deceitful religious offering men an apparent solution for all their problems at the expense of renunciation of the truth. That truth is the salvation that comes down from the Cross. The deception is continually present in the Church's history. Man is tempted to save himself without Christ, the Savior. But there is a special time when the deception reveals itself in a particular way. The *Catechism of the Catholic Church* (CCC) says: "The supreme religious deception is that of the Antichrist, a pseudo-messianism by which man glorifies himself in place of God and of his Messiah come in the flesh" (675).

These are truly illuminating words for they define the core of this deception which proposes a false salvation. This is the point, in synthesis, of Soloviev's *Tale* and of Benson's *Lord of the World*. Both writers present the Antichrist in the form of a humanitarian religion in which man, having excluded God, attempts his own salvation.

> The Antichrist's deception already begins to take shape in the world every time the claim is made to realize within history that messianic hope which can only be realized beyond history through the eschatological judgment. The Church has rejected even modified forms of this falsification of the kingdom to come under the name of millenarianism, especially the "intrinsically perverse" political form of a secular messianism. (CCC 676)

The Church on earth is a pilgrim and crucified Church. Hence there will be no thousand-year kingdom. Perhaps there will be times in which men will be more faithful to God than they are at present. More provocative is article 677:

> The Church will enter the glory of the kingdom only through this final Passover, [that is, the persecution or crucifixion that will take place at the time of the supreme deception] when she will follow her Lord in his death and Resurrection. The kingdom will be fulfilled, then, not by a historical triumph of the Church through a progressive ascendancy, but only by God's victory over the final unleashing of evil, which will cause his Bride to come down from heaven. God's triumph over the revolt of evil will take the form of the Last Judgment after the final cosmic upheaval of this passing world.

There will be a final attack made by the supreme Antichrist, Satan, and by his forces which are his historical incarnation, at the time of the great deception. At that time, as Jesus says, many will lose the faith: "When the Son of Man comes, will he find any faith on earth?" (Luke 18:8). At that time the world will come to an end. The final assault of evil will come to an end, although it will remain a part of history until then.

This is an outline of biblical and Church teaching about the Antichrist. He is an element, as Cardinal Biffi underlines, which is certainly part of the Christian message. This introduction tries to provide a necessary key by which to read Soloviev's *Tale of the Antichrist*, of which we spoke when referring to Cardinal Biffi's interview, and Benson's *Lord of the World*, which will be the subject of the second chapter of this book.

The clear teaching of the Bible, when interpreted according to the doctrine of the Church and not fantastically, is a certainty. Soloviev and Benson have a value, however, because of their capacity to discern whether today's world and its outlook do not in some way reflect those themes found in the Bible.

Others have written on this subject, apart from Soloviev and Benson. This makes it all the more necessary to have criteria with which to evaluate such writings.

The Antichrist by Vladimir Soloviev

Our choice of Soloviev's text—and our comment on it—can be explained by quoting from a foreword to the *Tale of the Antichrist*, published in *Il Sabato* (n. 14, April 2, 1988) which well illustrates its relevance today.

> One reason that urges us to introduce our readers to Soloviev's *Tale of the Antichrist* might be described as an impending sense of the approach of the end. "There is a great uneasiness," declared Paul VI towards the close of his pontificate, "at the present time, in the Church and in the world, and the faith is called into question. At this time, I am reminded of the strange phrase used by Jesus in St. Luke's Gospel: 'When the Son of Man comes will he find any faith on earth?' Are we approaching the end? This we shall never know. We have to be prepared, but it could be for a long while yet."
>
> Clearly, we are not speaking of a chronological end. Rather we are referring to a characteristic of modern life, which, as John Paul II notes in his last encyclical, "gives the impression of being subject to accelerating speed." This reflects a certain awareness of an end time which

The Wrath of God

Romano Guardini,[5] in his *La fine dell'epoca moderna*, describes in terms of dramatic conflict between Christ and the world—or non-faith. In 1950 Guardini wrote: "If we speak of the approaching end, it is intended not in a temporal sense but in an essential sense."

Paradoxically, the dramatic conflict between Christ and the world is not seen today in terms of an open or spectacular confrontation of the Catholic faith with the world. Perhaps certain revolutionaries' ideals of the 1960s would have foreseen a direct frontal engagement between the faith and the world—even if the best non-Catholic commentators of the period were in broad agreement with Paul VI's diagnosis. Giuseppe Prezzolini,[6] for example, wrote of the "liquidation of the Church": "This is the way to become one of the many Protestant sects." In 1969, Raymond Aron[7] saw that rapid secularization of the Catholic Church was a fact which would have greater consequences for civilization than all the agitation of that turbulent period.

Hence, the apparently fast approaching reckoning between Christ and His opponents will not be played out in a dramatic conflict but in an attempt to impoverish the Church from within in an attempt to liquidate it. The extermination of the Church will be sought not by means of persecution but by seduction which will result in a secularized Church.

In the 1980s an evident peace reigned between the great empires. The final struggle begins to assume forms and

[5] A theologian of Italian origin who lived in Germany (1885–1968).
[6] Writer and essayist (Perugia, 1882–Lugano, 1982).
[7] Notable French sociologist.

images already foreseen by Benson's novel *Lord of the World* and Soloviev's parable. The emperor, who represents worldly power for Soloviev, needs the services of the Church to achieve absolute and uncontested dominion. But this is a Church which, in some sense, has become a spiritual and moral agent of power so as to "cover over" (in a Protestant fashion) man's divisions and his radical unhappiness, without ever redly trying to save him. Soloviev's emperor encourages all Christian confessions to show sincere love which, at first sight, seems extremely generous. He gives Protestants the greatest school of "biblical studies" ever founded; the Orthodox are granted a museum of Christian archeology in veneration of "sacred tradition." To Catholics, the emperor intends to entrust the task of assuring "the proper spiritual order as well as that moral discipline which is indispensable for all."

In response to the emperor's proposals, the starets[8] declares: "Great Sovereign, for us the most precious thing in Christianity is Jesus Christ himself and all that comes from Him, since we know that the plenitude of divinity dwells corporeally in Him.... Confess, here and now before us, that Jesus Christ is the Son of God, that He became incarnate and rose from the dead; confess this and we shall receive you with love." Addressing him thus, the starets startled the emperor and, at that moment, the few remaining faithful followers of Pope Peter II recognized the emperor as the Antichrist.

So great is the Antichrist's power of seduction over believers—and they never realize it—that he will openly pose as the as the savior

[8] A representative of the Orthodox religion, an elder.

and restorer of religion and universal peace. He will deceive many. The real problem is to be able to recognize the Antichrist or the Antichrists present in every age, as St. John warns (1 John 4:3; 2 John 7).

> In the quotation cited earlier, Paul VI maintained that "It is enough if only a tiny flock, no matter how small, survives." How does Soloviev define the tiny flock?
>
> In Soloviev, the remnant is defined by recognition of Jesus Christ, "Himself and all that comes from Him." This is their total horizon and the inexhaustible meaning of life. The tiny flock is not made up of the avant-garde intelligentsia—the intellectuals and the theologians have joined the emperor. Neither are they defined in terms of a moral code. Rather they are those who refuse to serve two masters.

I tend to regard them as ordinary people, the humble, and those who remain faithful.

> The starets's profession is the narrative apex of the tale of the Antichrist and is the principle by which the Church exists in the world. It is the benchmark for society. Any society which does not permit the existence of this unexpected, and for some, inexplicable, tiny flock is neither democratic nor tolerant. Such societies only permit entities which have already been assimilated or can be assimilated by political power.

Vladimir Soloviev

Before reading from his beautiful parable, written just a century ago, we must mention something of the life of Vladimir Soloviev.

The Antichrist *by Vladimir Soloviev*

This great Russian writer was born Orthodox but, as we shall see, died Catholic, having embraced the Catholic Byzantine rite.

Vladimir Soloviev was born in Moscow in 1853. His was a profoundly Orthodox Christian family. While still a child he experienced an illumination of "Sofia," the Wisdom of God. While at school he became a materialist, an atheist, a socialist, and finally abandoned the religion of his youth. This was fashionable at the time. He studied various philosophers (Spinoza, Kant, Schelling, Schopenhauer, Comte). Eventually he formed a negative judgment of Western philosophy and of modern culture in general. He returned to the Orthodox faith in 1872. While studying at the Faculty of Philosophy, he began to attend the Ecclesiastical Academy of Moscow. He transferred to the University of St. Petersburg where he came into contact with some of the leading thinkers of his age. He became a close friend of the great Russian writer, Fyodor Mikhailovich Dostoevsky.

His courageous critique of the dominant philosophical currents of his time stemmed from his conviction that Christianity contained complete truth and was capable of transforming the world. This was the age which fermented the ideas which would eventually lead to atheistic Marxism. Soloviev, already swimming against the tide, was a courageous witness for the faith. Disillusioned by the Orthodox Church, he began a study of the ecumenical councils. He was drawn to the Catholic Church and arrived at the conclusion that Rome was truly Christian because it was truly universal. He took upon himself the task of promoting unification of the two Churches but, realizing the impossibility of this mission, he formally converted to Catholicism and embraced the Byzantine rite. He died on July 31, 1900, praying in Hebrew for the Jews. His writings include ten volumes of philosophical writings, one of poetry, and numerous letters.

The Wrath of God

As we can see, Soloviev was a man of great philosophical and theological learning. He understood the faith and bore courageous witness to it in the midst of the errors of his day. He was not a novelist. He used the Antichrist as a parable to express, in the light of Divine Wisdom, his own "sofia," or wisdom, and his intuition of the character of the age in which he lived. His philosophical and theological research brought him to conversion to the Catholic Church which is like a seal set on a life particularly marked by the light of Divine Wisdom. His prophetic power, amply demonstrated in his *Tale*, is especially interesting for Catholics.

Let us now read some of the more important passages of this short work written between 1899 and 1900.[9]

Portrait of a Superman

There lived at that time a remarkable man — many called him a superman — who was as far from being a child in intellect as in heart.

I must comment on this text since it is one of the most intelligent, acute, and profound pieces ever written about the Antichrist. Soloviev defines the Antichrist fundamentally in terms of presumption and pride. He possesses all the moral and spiritual qualities. He is highly intelligent and an ascetic. But he is not humble and hence subject to becoming a Son of Satan. With exceptional intuition, Soloviev understood the depths of the Gospel.

He was young, but his genius made him widely famous as a great thinker, writer and social worker by the time he was

---

[9] The text of Soloviev's tale and Benson's novel are quoted in italics while Fr. Livio's interventions are printed in toto.

thirty-three. Conscious of his own great spiritual power, he had always been a convinced idealist, and his clear intelligence always made clear to him the truth of that which ought to be believed in: the good, God, the Messiah.

The key point of Soloviev's portrait of the Antichrist is the satisfying awareness which the future Antichrist has of his own greatness and his own spiritual power. In contrast, the saints sincerely regard themselves as sinners and generally do not know that they are saints. But the Antichrist was a man who was completely open to spiritual values. He understood them all except one—humility. He knew nothing of littleness and childlikeness. In truth, however,

> he loved only himself. He believed in God, but at the bottom of his heart unconsciously and instinctively preferred himself to Him. He believed in the Good, but the all-seeing Eye of Eternity knew that he would bow down before the powers of evil, as soon as it had corrupted him, not by appealing to his senses, base passions or to the supreme temptation of power, but by caressing his boundless pride.

It is striking that the Evil One could not corrupt the Antichrist by flattering his baser instincts with promises of money, gratification of the senses, or the prospect of power. Instead he manipulated his boundless pride. He had good reason to be full of himself. Here was a man who possessed high intellectual and moral gifts combined with a nobility and grace of aspect which made him a spiritualist, an ascetic, and a philanthropist who was not prey to the baser instincts. He was generous to mankind and amply justified in his own limitless self-admiration.

Soloviev well reflects St. Paul's man of iniquity, the Antichrist who presents himself as God and demands to be worshipped as God (2 Thess. 2:4). At a human level, the portrait mirrors the interior events which transformed Lucifer into the angel of evil: Lucifer, the most beautiful of all God's angels, contemplating himself, fell in love with himself and eventually preferred himself to God. A similar process takes place in the central character of the *Tale*. He saw the characteristics of Christ in himself.

He regarded the abundance of gifts he had received from God as a sign of special heavenly favor. This conviction did not engender any gratitude to God in him or service to his neighbor. Rather it led him to believe that he was superior to all others, including Christ, by right.

At the beginning he had no hostility against Jesus. He admitted his messianic dignity[10] and significance, but he sincerely saw in him merely the greatest of his own predecessors; his mind, clouded by pride, could not understand Christ's moral achievement and his absolute uniqueness. He reasoned thus: "Christ came before me; I come second; but that which in the order of time comes later is essentially prior. I come last, at the end of history, just because I am the perfect and final savior. The first Christ was my forerunner. His mission was to anticipate and prepare my coming." With this idea in his mind the great man of the twenty-first century applied to himself all that is said in the Gospels about the second coming, understanding by it, not

[10] The Hebrew etymology of the term "messiah" is "anointed," hence the Greek equivalent "Christ," which of itself does not indicate divinity.

the return of the same Christ, but the replacement of the
preliminary Christ by the final, that is, by himself.

The Antichrist regarded himself as the true and definitive Christ.

According to Soloviev the Antichrist will appear at the transi-
tion from the second to the third millennium. This is strangely
analogous with Benson's vision which, although written at the
beginning of this century, situates the appearance of the Antichrist
at the end of this century.

Up to that point the "man of the future" was still clearly
defined and original. He regarded Christ in much the same
way as Mahomet, a just man to whom no evil intention
could be imputed.

Mahomet regarded Christ as a prophet but believed that the
one who followed him was the Christ. As with Mahomet, the
Antichrist regards Christ as his precursor.

This man also justified his proud preference of himself to
Christ by the following argument: "Christ, in preaching the
moral good and manifesting it in his life, was the reformer
of mankind, but I am destined to be the benefactor of this
partly reformed, partly incorrigible mankind. I shall give all
men what they need. Christ as a moralist divided men into
the good and the bad, but I will unite them by blessings
which are needed by the good and bad alike. I shall be the
true representative of the God who makes His sun to rise
on the evil and on the good and sends rain on the just and
the unjust. Christ brought a sword, I shall bring peace. He
threatened the earth with the dreadful last judgment. But
I shall be the last judge, and my judgment shall be one of
mercy as well as of justice."

The Antichrist Will Free Us from Hell

"There will be justice too in my judgment, not retributive, but distributive justice. I will make distinctions between people and give everyone their due."

In this beautiful frame of mind he waited for some clear call from God, for some manifest and striking testimony to his being the eldest son, God's beloved first-born. He waited, and meanwhile nurtured his selfhood on the contemplation of his superhuman gifts and virtues—as already said, he was a man of irreproachable morality and extraordinary genius. This righteous and proud man waited and waited for a sanction from above to begin his work of saving humanity—and still the sanction did not come.

In summary, Soloviev's Antichrist possesses all intellectual and moral qualities, but lacks a childlike intelligence and heart so as to be humble before God. He does not have the childlikeness of which Christ speaks when He says that no one can enter the Kingdom of Heaven unless he become like a little child (cf. Matt. 18:3-4).

Let us now examine the interior fall which brought the Antichrist to raise himself up to the level of God. Apart from a lack of humility, the Antichrist gradually came to believe that he was greater than Christ and eventually proclaimed himself God. Such a psychological process could not have progressed to its end unless it were specifically encouraged by Satan who makes the Antichrist his chosen son.

Climbing to the Level of God

Benson and Soloviev characterize the Antichrist as aping Christ.

The Evil One's attempt to imitate God is expressly mentioned by St. Paul when he says that Satan likes to present himself in the form of an angel of light (2 Cor. 11:14). Revelation points to the same idea when it speaks of the two beasts who serve the dragon and the lamb (Rev. 13:11). These ideas are rooted in the teaching of Christ on false prophets. They clothe themselves as sheep but in truth they are ravaging wolves (Matt. 7:15).

Benson understood this biblical teaching very well and held that the external appearance of the Antichrist was in every way identical with the Pope of the time. It was difficult for those who knew them personally to distinguish them.

Soloviev maintains the same idea in his *Tale* with the Antichrist portrayed as a young man. He was the same age as Christ when he accomplished our redemption: thirty-three. The Antichrist's age is especially significant and suggests a human version of Christ who is the Christ of this world.

Let us examine the spiritual decline of this great genius of a just man who is full of pride but morally reprehensible. He believes in God but loves nobody but himself. His relationship with Christ was quickly defined as one of superiority, in that while Christ was the Redeemer of man, he would be man's benefactor. While Christ brought the sword, he would bring peace.

> He was thirty-three years old already; another three years passed. And suddenly there flashed through his mind a thought that sent a hot tremor into the very marrow of his bones: "And what if ...? What if not I, but that other ... the Galilean ...? What if He is not my forerunner, but the real one, the first and the last? But then He must be living ... Where is He? ... What if He comes to me ... here, now ... What shall I say to Him? Why, I shall have to bow before Him like the most stupid of Christians, shall have to mutter senselessly like a Russian peasant, 'Lord Jesus Christ, have

mercy on me,' or grovel like a Polish countrywoman! I, the bright genius, the superman! No, never!"

This is a marvelous passage, for it well illustrates the real obstacle to salvation. Man cannot be saved as long as he refuses to recognize his sinful condition. This is a sin against the Holy Spirit. Unbounded pride atrophies the heart when man refuses to recognize his sinful condition and Christ his Savior. His only preoccupation, suspicion, and fear is that Christ may truly be the Son of God before Whom he would have to prostrate himself and Whom he would have to accept as Savior.

The Sin of Lucifer

And instead of the former cold rational respect for God and Christ there was born and grew in his heart, first, a kind of terror, and then a burning, choking and corroding envy and furious, breath-taking hatred. "I, I, and not He! He is not living, He is not and shall not be. He is not risen, He is not risen from the dead! He rotted in the tomb, rotted like the lowest."

The Antichrist, as described by Soloviev, suffers the same envy of God that transformed Lucifer, the most beautiful of the angels, into a demon, Satan. Transposed into human terms, this same envy animates the Antichrist in his relationship with Christ. The sin of Lucifer was that he could not abide the idea that God existed since he wished to become God. The Antichrist's sin consists in being unable to tolerate the idea that a greater man than himself exists, namely Christ. The very suspicion that Christ might be greater than he engenders envy in him and consequently revolt and radical opposition to Christ. Hence, he is defined as the Antichrist.

Pride and envy, as we have seen, are the common bonds linking Satan, the Antichrist *par excellence*, with the Antichrist, his representative on earth. God is God and we are creatures.

What squalor is to be seen in the sin of Lucifer and the Antichrist and in those who have been infected with the same venom of the serpent! God has the untried pleasure—since it is impossible for Him—of not being a creature, something small. It is such a joy for man to realize that he is such a small creature, and that God, not being able to experience this joy as God, became a child ... and we, like children, are carried in His arms and sleep quietly in His breast. The proud reject this joy, the infinite joy of being small, of being a creature.

The Antichrist, devoured with envy of Christ, cries out:

"He rotted in the tomb, rotted like the lowest ... " Foaming at the mouth, he rushed out of the house and garden and, leaping and bounding, ran in the black depth of the night along the rocky path ... The fury died down, and despair, hard and heavy as the rocks and dark as the night, took its place. He stopped at the sheer drop of the cliff and heard the vague noise of the stream rushing along the stones far below. Unendurable anguish weighed on his heart. Suddenly, something stirred within him. "Shall I call Him—ask Him what I am to do?" And the sad and gentle image seemed to rise before him in the darkness.

It is the face of Christ, the Good Shepherd, who has compassion for the lost sheep. The Antichrist cannot tolerate Christ's existence or his compassion for him.

"He pities me ... No, never! He did not, he did not rise from the dead!" And he threw himself down from the cliff. But something resilient like a water-spout supported him in the air, he felt a kind of electric shock, and some power flung him back. He lost consciousness for a moment and when he came to himself he was kneeling a few steps away from the edge of the cliff. He saw the outline of a figure glowing with a misty phosphorescent light and its eyes penetrated his soul with their intolerable sharp brilliance.

The most important thing in anyone's life, and not just in the Antichrist's, is that mysterious moment when Christ knocks at the door and offers His love, His pardon, and His friendship. At this very moment the Evil One begins his work of temptation.

He saw those piercing eyes and heard—he did not know whether from within himself or from outside—a strange voice, toneless and, as it were, stifled, and yet clear, metallic and absolutely soulless as though coming from a phonograph.

The description of Satan, especially his aspect and his voice, is very effective and suggestive. Those who, in one way or another, have had an experience of him through the practice of magic or for some other reason, will recognize Soloviev's accuracy of description. St. Ignatius mentions in his autobiography that he had had a similar experience of the Evil One. He mentions the clarity of his aspect and two deep, black pools of eyes that stared at him.

Satan's Argument

And the voice was saying to him: "You are my beloved son in whom I am well pleased. Why have you not sought me?

Why did you revere that other, the bad one, and His Father?
I am your god and your father."

Satan's argument is very similar to the one he used with Adam
and Eve in the garden. Typically, Satan regards himself as God.
He is good. "Others" are evil.

"And that other one, the beggar, the crucified, is a stranger
both to me and to you. I have no other son but you. You
are my only one, only begotten, co-equal with me."

With great geniality, Soloviev places the Antichrist on the same level
as Christ. From there he deploys his opposition to Christ. As Christ
was begotten by God and the Word made flesh, in Soloviev's parable
Satan begets this creature. While a creature of God, the Antichrist is
spiritually generated by Satan in that he communicates his own spirit
to him. That spirit is characterized by its opposition to God. It is a
negative representation of that unique paternity which characterizes
the relationship between God the Father and Christ the Son. Satan
has a similar relationship with the Antichrist, for the Antichrist
has become his beloved son. It is interesting to note that this idea
is also found in the tradition of mystical writers. Satan continues:

"I have no envy, I love you. I want nothing from you. You
are beautiful, powerful and great. Do your work in your
own name, not in mine."

In Soloviev, Satan's discourse is the mirror opposite of Christ's.
While God asks for man's total self-giving, Satan urges him to a
total affirmation of himself. The consequences of self-affirmation
were predicted by Christ: "Anyone who wants to save his life will
lose it; but anyone who loses his life for my sake, and for the sake
of the gospel, will save it" (cf. Mark 8:35; Matt. 10:39; Luke 17:33).

"I am not envious of you." Echoing Genesis (3:4–5), Solo-viev makes clear reference to Satan's telling Adam and Eve that God forbade them from eating of the fruit of the tree because He feared they would become like Him.

I wonder how Soloviev could have written this passage without having had some personal spiritual experience which gave him an intuition of the subtlety with which Satan corrupts and falsifies the truth.

Satan Pours Out His Spirit

"I ask nothing of you, and I will help you. I will help you for your own sake, for the sake of your own dignity and excellence and of my pure disinterested love for you. Receive my spirit. Once upon a time my spirit gave birth to you in beauty, now it gives birth to you in power." At these words of the unknown being the superman's lips opened of themselves, two piercing eyes came quite close to his face, and he felt a sharp, frozen stream enter into him and fill his whole being. And at the same time he was conscious of a wonderful strength, energy, lightness and rapture. At that instant the luminous outline and the eyes suddenly disappeared, something lifted him into the air and at once deposited him in the garden by the house door.

At this point, a striking contrast is noticeable: while the apostle who receives the power of God is full of wisdom and courage (cf. the letters of St. Paul), he remains a crucified apostle. Those, how-ever, who receive the power of the devil, like the devil are tireless in their activities. Sometimes we are hesitant, brokenhearted, or slow to do good while it is a marvel to behold the agility and frenetic industry with which others devote themselves to discovering new ways of doing evil. From where does all this energy and geniality come? It is generated by the spirit of the Evil One who is tireless in doing evil. His spirit pervades those whom he urges: "Receive my spirit. I beget you in my power."

Satanic Investiture and Worldly Success

We have seen that the crucial point in the life of the Antichrist was his rejection of the meekness and compassion of Christ and his acceptance of Satan's promise which flattered his pride.

Satan had found well-prepared soil. It is easy for Satan to enter a proud heart and take possession of it. What happened to the Antichrist in a unique and unrepeatable way took place on a large scale. But ultimately, it is exactly what happens to all of us. Soloviev's drama could happen to any one of us.

When the Antichrist becomes the chosen son of Satan and permeates his heart with the outlook of Satan, since he had been begotten by his power and infused with the spirit of evil, he begins to experience unbelievable worldly success.

An important lesson can be learned from this. The world is under the dominion of the "Prince of this world." Outstanding success without setbacks, opposition, or persecution—without ever being targeted—is extremely alarming, for it could imply being an adept of the Evil One. For those who work for God and the Church, worldly success can never be an adequate reference point or an acceptable yardstick. Oftentimes, lack of success and persecution can be sure signs that you stand for God.

Soloviev describes all the worldly success of his Antichrist. As if driven by some superhuman force, he writes a work which is at once popular and overwhelming. The title is significant: *The Open Way to Universal Peace and Welfare.*

The Wrath of God

Politician with Religious Concerns

Eschewing this or that alleged private revelation, we approach this subject from the perspective of those who have studied these phenomena. We note that for Soloviev, Benson, and others, the Antichrist is a layman engaged in politics who portrays himself as a great savior and benefactor of mankind. As we shall soon see, he combines political activity with religious concerns — indeed he even convokes an Ecumenical Council. Other recent writers on the subject of the Antichrist (Maria Valtorta) describe him as an ecclesiastic who belongs to the priestly cast.

Reconciliation of Opposites

Soloviev's Antichrist writes his book which quickly becomes famous. He had written others, but they had been indifferently received, especially in religious circles where they were criticized for their presumptuous tone. His new work, however, had the signs of rare genius. It was successful in every intellectual undertaking and in accomplishing its most difficult philosophical objectives.

The secret of its success lay in its extraordinary power of synthesis which supported no particular thesis or truth but reconciled all truths, opinions, philosophies and religions. Soloviev defined it as "something which understands and conciliates all contradictions." The Antichrist presents himself as the great conciliator and mediator. He has the capacity to erect his truth into a synthesis of all partial truths produced by man in the course of history. Religious truth is also regarded as a product of human history. The synthesis of the Antichrist includes the truths of Catholics, Protestants, the Orthodox, and even of the atheists. It will accommodate both traditionalists and progressives. Left, right, and center will be satisfied because the amalgam contained in the synthesis of diversity will contain something which is pleasing to everyone. The Antichrist's book can be interpreted from whatever point of view is acceptable to his readers since it gives the impression that it was written especially to vindicate their very own positions.

> It was all-embracing and all-reconciling. It combined noble reverence for ancient traditions and symbols with broad and bold radicalism in social and political demands and precepts, boundless freedom of thought with the deepest understanding of all things mystical, absolute individualism with ardent devotion to the common good, the most lofty idealism of guiding principles with thoroughly definite and concrete practical conclusions. And it was all put together with such consummate art that every one-sided thinker or reformer could easily see and accept the whole entirely from his own particular point of view, without sacrificing anything for *the truth itself.*

The book is an instant success and is widely circulated. Its author wins instant and universal notoriety.

No one raised objections against this book, for it seemed to everyone a revelation of the all-embracing truth. It did such complete justice to the past, it passed such dispassionate judgment on every aspect of the present, it brought the better future so concretely and tangibly within reach, that everyone said: "This is the very thing we want; here is an ideal that is not utopian, a plan which is not a chimera." The wonderful writer carried all with him and was acceptable to everyone, so that Christ's words were fulfilled. "I am come in my Father's name, and ye receive me not: if another shall come in his own name, him ye will receive."[11] For in order to be received, one must be acceptable.

This is truly a radical reversal. Christ is rejected by the world along with His mission. The world's final word to Him is the cross. (We will crucify you because you are a troublemaker.) The world reacts differently to the Antichrist. It applauds and welcomes him. It crowns him and offers tribute to him. The words of Christ are disturbing and upset life ("It is not peace I have come to bring, but a sword" [Matt. 10:34]) because even natural bonds are sundered by their absoluteness. The Antichrist conciliates all. He succeeds in ushering in a period of universal concord, not only among men, but also between rival social, political, economic, and ideological systems. His mark is the mark of success and glory.

The Little Flock

The success of the Antichrist is almost universal. Only a tiny minority is perplexed by his proposals. (Here we are reminded of Paul VI: "A tiny flock must remain.")

It does not appear strange to the majority of Christians that the name of Christ is never mentioned in the Antichrist's book. Rather benevolence and universal love, which are essential Christian virtues, are the only important things. Soloviev points out that such a reply restores concord among all.

The Mission of the Antichrist

Antichrist's mission begins at this point. He has achieved success with his book. It jumbled together in a pleasing way many

[11] Cf. John 5:43.

ingredients produced by man in the course of history. The time now comes to put his plan into action.

Soloviev envisages the Antichrist's activities as operative on several different levels. At a political level the Antichrist brings universal peace, since he is the man of peace. On a social level, he is the great reformer who succeeds in eradicating poverty.

As a pacifist and social reformer, Soloviev's Antichrist is identical with Benson's. Both writers show substantial agreement in their portrayal of the Antichrist as the one who would ensure world peace and prosperity for man, whose history has been devastated by war and scourged by misery. The Antichrist is the true savior of man.

More interesting again is the Antichrist's attitude to the Church and to religions.

The Political Plan

The first part of the Antichrist's plan is political in character. Soloviev imagines the creation of a union of the states of Europe which arrives at the point of collapse because of friction between its members. Masonry (which counts the political leaders and those who hold and manipulate political power among its adepts) is determined to avoid this threat by entrusting full executive power to one of its secret members who is none other than our protagonist, "the man of the future." He possesses all the qualifications necessary for high authority: scientific competence, influential social position, and universal acclaim following the recent publication of his book.

> The man of the future was elected almost unanimously lifelong president of the United States of Europe. When he appeared on the rostrum in all the brilliance of his

superhuman young strength and beauty and, with inspired
eloquence, expounded his universal program, the assembly,
charmed and completely carried away, in a burst of enthusiasm decided without putting it to a vote to pay him the
highest tribute by electing him Roman Emperor.

At this point attention could be given to a characteristic of the
Antichrist which remains in the background of both Benson's and
Soloviev's portrayal but which would become apparent with all its
force at the opportune time.

Much discussion has been devoted to the question of whether
the Antichrist is a collective moment or a person. Soloviev and
Benson regard him as both. I believe that it is symptomatic that both
Soloviev and Benson, who treat this subject prophetically, hold that
the person of the Antichrist is an expression of international Masonry whose plan is to rid the world of war, hunger, and ignorance
by making of mankind one great family ruled by the light of reason.

This is substantially the objective of international Masonry.
Among other things, it envisages the reduction of all religious
experience to a single common denominator which is found in
a form of natural religion. Benson called this humanitarianism.
Soloviev conceived of it as an attempt to unite the various Christian churches once they have been purged of faith in Jesus Christ.

Soloviev regards the Antichrist as a secret member of international Masonry and its instrument for the realization of its ideals.
It pursues the creation of a world in which man will save himself by
his own capacities. The personal qualities of the Antichrist and the
assistance given to him by the Evil One allow him to advance the
plan of autosalvation which eliminates the need for God's assistance.

Masonry helps the Antichrist to succeed in his plans for universal peace. Nation states are superseded by fraternity among men.

The pacifism of this plan is achieved by the creation of a central coercive force which imposes peace on all.

> The assembly closed amidst general rejoicing, and the great elect published a manifesto beginning with the words "Peoples of the Earth! My Peace I give unto You" and ending as follows: "The Promises have been fulfilled! Eternal universal peace is secured. Every attempt to disturb it shall be immediately met with overwhelming opposition.... Henceforth no country will dare say 'war' when I say 'peace.' Nations of the world, peace be unto you!"

This, as we can see, is an aping and a mockery of the words of Christ: "My own peace I give you." Christ added: "a peace the world cannot give" (John 14:27). The Antichrist, however, gives the "peace" of the world.

> The manifesto had the desired effect. Everywhere outside of Europe, especially in America, there was strong support for the empire. Governments were forced to unite, on different conditions, with the United States of Europe, under the supreme rule of the Roman Emperor. In Asia and Africa some tribes and some sovereigns still remained independent. The Emperor, with a small but well-chosen army of Russian, Polish and Hungarian troops [all armies that had fought each other during the course of history], undertook a military campaign stretching from east Asia to Morocco. Without great fighting or bloodshed the last diehards were reduced to his obedience.

Wars are like intelligently used explosives: major victories won with minimal bloodshed (as far as the imperial troops are concerned, since the number of dead on the opposing side counts for nothing).

A Lightning Success
In all the states on both sides of the world, he appointed governors, chosen from the local magnates who had been educated in Europe and who were loyal to him. In all these pagan countries, the populations regarded him as a superior divinity.

The kingdom of the Antichrist is not like the Kingdom of God which slowly grows. Like a seed, it is planted, remains underground where it ferments and gradually develops. The Antichrist, however, realizes his plans immediately and his kingdom grows with frightening speed. This is typical of the Devil. He craves the affirmation of the world with colossal stunts.

Within a year a worldwide monarchy in the exact and proper sense of the term was founded. The seedlings of war were pulled out by the roots.

War is really rooted in man's heart. This fact is not mentioned here. The personality of the Emperor is sufficient to assure peace.

The League of Universal Peace met for the last time and, having addressed an enthusiastic eulogy to the great peacemaker, dissolved itself as no longer necessary.

The Social Plan
Man is troubled by problems from three great sources: political, social, and religious. We have seen the rapidity with which the Antichrist resolved political problems. Following the institution of universal peace, we shall see the acuteness, speed and acumen with which he tackled social problems. Trade unions and industrial actions will no longer be necessary.

In the second year of his reign the Roman and universal emperor issued another manifesto: "Peoples of the earth! I promised you peace and I have given it to you. But peace is only made sweet by prosperity. It is no joy to those who are threatened with destitution. Come unto me, all you that are cold and hungry and I will give you food and warmth."

These words clearly ape those of Christ. While Christ gives living water, the Antichrist can only provide a surrogate (that which article 675 of the *Catechism of the Catholic Church* significantly calls "an apparent solution" to man's problems).

> Then he announced a simple and all-inclusive social reform that was already indicated in his book and had captivated at the time all noble and clear minds. Now that the world's finances and enormous landed properties were concentrated in his hands, he could carry out this reform and satisfy the desires of the poor without appreciable injustice to the rich. Everyone was paid according to his capacity, and every capacity was rewarded according to its merits and results.

The Antichrist will succeed where both communism and trade-unionism failed. He will give peace and bread to everybody. What more could one ask for? At the time of the Antichrist men will think to themselves that "finally a serious person has come who can provide for our well-being on earth." "What do we want Christ for, since we are so well off with the Antichrist here on earth?"

Animalism

The Antichrist is the friend of animals. He is a vegetarian. He assures the wellbeing not only of men but also of animals. This is an aspect of the Antichrist's plan which is remarkably striking because of its current relevance.

The new Lord of the Earth was a philanthropist, full of compassion. Not only was he a friend of man but he was also a friend of animals. [I am certain that this will be seen as an irrefutable argument by many readers.] He was a vegetarian. He forbade vivisection and ordered slaughter-houses to be strictly controlled. He encouraged a society which protected animals in every way.

Boredom of Universal Satiation

There was firmly established in all mankind the most important form of equality—the equality of general satiety. That was done in the second year of his reign. The social and economic problem was solved once and for all. But though food is of first importance to the hungry, those who have sufficient food want something else. Even the animals when they had enough to eat want not merely to sleep but to play as well. This is even more true of men who post *panem* have also demanded *circences*.

All are obliged to be well in the Antichrist's society. Both men and animals are at peace and have full stomachs. The Antichrist, however, notices that when man is at peace he becomes bored. Soloviev here develops a theme of St. Paul's second letter to the Thessalonians which holds that the Antichrist will come with the power of Satan and work many wonders (2 Thess. 2:9). Soloviev's Antichrist does not work wonders himself since he has deputed this work to an apostate Catholic bishop. (This could be regarded as a piece of anti-Catholic polemic since we should not forget that Soloviev had been Orthodox). The apostate Catholic bishop is called Apollonius and is a kind of magician. He performs many prodigies and miracles with which the Antichrist fascinates, entertains, and astonishes mankind.

The superhuman-emperor understood what the crowd needed. At that time a great magician surrounded with a halo of strange facts and wild fairy-tales came to him in Rome from the distant East. The magician, Appollonius by name, unquestionably a man of genius, was a Catholic bishop *in partibus infidelium*. He combined in a marvelous way a mastery of the latest discoveries and technical application of Western science with a knowledge both theoretical and practical of all that is real and significant in the traditional mysticism of the East. The results of this combination were astounding.

Given its current relevance, it is highly interesting that Soloviev should have Apollonius unite eastern mysticism and western technology.

Apollonius mastered, for instance, the half-scientific and half-magical art of attracting and directing at his will atmospheric electricity, so that people said he commanded fire to come down from heaven.

Let us not forget that this is one of the traits ascribed by the Bible to the Antichrist (Rev. 13:13).

But while striking the imagination of the multitude by all kinds of unheard-of novelties he refrained for a time from abusing his power for any special purposes. And so this man came to the great emperor, worshipped him as the true son of God, and, declaring that in the secret books of the East he had found direct prophecies about him as the last savior and judge of the earth, offered himself and his art in service to him.

Soloviev also refers to chapter 13 of the book of Revelation which speaks of the beast which resembles a panther — symbol of political power—and the beast resembling a lamb—symbol of the religious power of the false prophet—which uses its satanic power to lead men to worship the panther, the Antichrist who represents political power.

> The emperor was charmed, accepted him as a gift from above, and bestowing splendid titles upon him, kept the magician permanently at his side. The peoples of the earth, having received from their master the blessings of universal peace and abundant food for all, were also given the chance of permanently enjoying the most diverse and unexpected signs and miracles. The third year of the superman's reign was coming to an end.

By the end of the first part of the *Tale,* we note that Soloviev has drawn a picture of the Antichrist which shows him to be anything but malicious. Rather he is a man of high intelligence and of eminent virtues. However, he is man who intends to raise his own "ego" above, or, at least, to the same level as God. This is his Achilles' heel and Satan manipulates it by proposing to adopt him as his son, thereby making him his representative on earth. From that moment, the Antichrist has the unconditional support of Satan. This very support ensured the universal success of his book *The Open Way to Universal Peace and Prosperity* and the putting into effect of his plan for the reform of mankind in the course of only three years. With universal peace the Antichrist becomes a great pacifist. Social reform ensures that every man and every animal has food. The Antichrist provides for the well-being of all. Finally, his plan for the "holiday industry" provides entertainment for all by the finest tricks that magic can produce. Thus, every nation on the face of the earth can be amused by the most unexpected magical illusions.

Thus, the first three years of the Antichrist's reign draw to a close. The Antichrist appears as the representative of Satan who desires to save man, in his own way, by guaranteeing him paradise on this earth.

In many ways Soloviev's *Tale* can be seen as an authentic anticipation of the *Catechism*. It is a denunciation of the worldly spirit which encourages man in the proud illusion that he is the author of his own salvation. In this perspective, religion is but one ingredient of earthly happiness.

This is the most important and decisive religious question to emerge in the *Tale* and is undoubtedly the most interesting part of Soloviev's work.

We have seen that in the first three years of his reign the Antichrist succeeds in establishing that which Christ has failed to establish for the past two thousand years — universal peace and social reform. Now the moment of crisis arrives.

There are in fact still believers who are divided between different religions. Soloviev pays special attention to the three components of Christianity: Catholicism, the Orthodox Church, and Protestantism. These begin to suspect that they are faced with someone who is trying to eradicate Christ from man's very heart. The Antichrist is forced to address the religious question in depth.

The Religious Question

Naturally, the Antichrist is immediately interested in Christianity because his objective is to eradicate Christ, after which he knows that he will have no difficulty in brushing away all other religions. At the time of the Antichrist the number of believers will be greatly reduced. In the whole world, Christians will number no more than forty-five million.

A great apostasy is taking place. The program of political and social reform, so successfully carried through, seems to satisfy man's every desire and need. Many are enchanted by the new religion of humanitarianism and have turned their backs on the faith. What the Gospel says of false prophets has come to pass (see Matt. 24:11ff; Mark 13:22). The greatest of these is the Antichrist.

The three Christian confessions—Catholicism, Protestantism, and Orthodoxy—are numerically much reduced but have approximately equal numbers of believers. Faced with the common threat of seduction their historical hostilities are more attenuated and they now have found a greater solidarity.

In these circumstances, the quality of the few remaining Christians is very high: "Men who had no spiritual interests in common with Christianity were no longer numbered among Christians."

Soloviev employs great imagination in describing the condition of each of the three Christian confessions.

Catholicism, while greatly reduced in numbers, still conserves its cosmopolitanism. It is still compact, well organized, and united under the Pope who no longer resides in Rome.

Papacy had long been exiled from Rome and after many wanderings had found shelter in St. Petersburg on condition that it was to refrain from propaganda, both there and within the country. In Russia it assumed a much simpler form. Without decreasing the necessary personnel of its colleges and offices, it had to spiritualize the nature of their activities, and also to bring down to a minimum its splendid ritual and ceremonial observances.

Compared with Soloviev's time, many of the rites and ceremonies of Catholicism have been modified so as to emphasize what is essential. The Papacy, while still in Rome, has assumed a more sober or Franciscan style.

Many strange customs that might be a stumbling block fell out of usage, though they were not formally abolished. In all other countries, especially in North America, the Roman Catholic hierarchy still had many representatives with an independent position, strong will and indefatigable energy; they made the unity of the Roman Church more closely knit than ever and preserved its international, cosmopolitan significance.

Indeed, one of the most beautiful characteristics of Catholicism, exemplified more clearly in no other religion, is its universality.

Protestantism, like Catholicism, is much reduced. Soloviev foresaw the unity of most Anglicans with Catholicism—something which has not yet happened. Protestantism becomes more profoundly rooted in the faith and ardent for the Gospel.

It had freed itself from its extreme negative tendencies whose champions openly passed over to religious indifference and unbelief. Only sincere believers remained in the Evangelical Church; the men who stood at the head of it combined wide erudition with deep religious faith, and strove more and more to become the living image of the true ancient Christianity. Russian Orthodoxy had lost many millions of its nominal members when political events changed the official position of the Church, but it had the joy of being united to the best elements among the Old Believers [the most militant among Orthodox believers] and even among many sectarians of the positively religious type. The regenerated Church, while not increasing in numbers, grew in spiritual power, which showed itself very clearly in the struggle against extremist sects with a demonic and satanic tinge that had multiplied both among the masses and in society.

It is truly extraordinary how Soloviev, writing a century ago, could highlight certain currents which now pervade society but which were then nascent—for example, Satanism.

This is the position of the three churches in the first three years of the Antichrist's reign. They are marked by numerical reduction of the faithful and a strong return to evangelical origins. The churches have become a tiny flock in which the Father causes the splendor of the Kingdom to shine.

Thus, Soloviev describes their relationship with the extraordinary man who, for the first time in history, has solved all of man's problems.

> During the first two years of the new reign the Christians' attitude toward the emperor and his peaceful reforms was one of definite sympathy and even enthusiasm. But in the third year, when the great magician appeared, many of the Orthodox, Catholics and Evangelicals began to feel uneasy and to disapprove. The passages in the Gospels and the Epistles about the prince of this world and the antichrist were read more attentively than before and excited lively comments.

Nobody yet realizes that the Emperor is the Antichrist. The Christians are about to discover it.

The Storm Intensifies

From certain signs the emperor guessed that a storm was gathering, and decided to make haste and clear up matters. Early in the fourth year of his reign he addressed a manifesto to all faithful Christians of whatever denomination, inviting them to elect or appoint plenipotentiary representatives to an ecumenical council under his presidency.

The Antichrist attempts to unite the Church and end all divisions among Christians. Finally, he, and not Christ, is savior of the Church because he succeeds where Christians failed in ecumenical dialogue.

The emperor transfers his residence to Jerusalem. There he builds an enormous temple destined for the worship of all religions. It becomes a tangible expression of the Antichrist's plan to banish wars of religion, competitive religions, and religions which spread discord among men.

Only one temple will be erected. It will be an imperial temple in which all religions will be united. But who will be adored in this temple? The man made god, the Antichrist, will be worshipped in this temple. The man of all religions will present himself as the sole object of worship. This is not far removed from what Daniel denounced as the abomination of desolation (cf. Dan. 9:27; 11:31; 12:11) and Paul warned of when he said that the son of perdition will come and "enthrone himself in God's sanctuary and claim that he is God" (2 Thess. 2:4).

Soloviev is more than a novelist. He is a great theologian who, like Benson, can communicate profound theological insights through the medium of novels and parables—such as his portrait of the Antichrist as one who will construct an imperial temple for the united worship of all religions.

The great temple is flanked by two sumptuous palaces, reserved for the emperor. They contain libraries, museums, and a home for those who experiment with and practice magic. Clearly Soloviev profoundly grasped many of the tendencies of modern society. This is evident, dear friends, when we recall that there are one hundred thousand magicians in Italy—twice the number of priests in the country. Fifteen million Italians consult them, which is more than the total of those who practice their religion. These people are already in the Antichrist's train. Even though not incarnate in any historical person, he is represented in the world by the spirit of the times. Soloviev's *Tale*, written a century ago, exhibits an extraordinary capacity to decipher the signs of the times.

> The ecumenical council was to open in this semi-temple and semi-palace on the fourteenth of September.[12] Since the Evangelical denomination had no priesthood in the proper sense, the Orthodox and Catholic hierarchs in accordance with the emperor's wishes decided, for the sake of uniformity among the delegates, to admit to the council some of their laymen known for their piety and devotion to the interests of the Church; and if laymen were admitted, the rank and file of the clergy and monks could not be excluded.

This is evidently a democratic Council, and its members are chosen according to the rules of modern democracy. It is not a Council which reflects the constitution given to the Church by Christ.

> Thus the general number of the council members exceeded three thousand, and about half a million Christian pilgrims flooded Jerusalem and Palestine. There were three outstanding men among the council members.

It should be clearly noted that this is not a valid Council. By a profane act it was convoked by the emperor and held in a temple dedicated to the unity of all religions and in the shadow of an edifice infested by magic. The Council is convoked by democratic principles so as to allow not only the bishops to participate but

---

[12] Significantly, Soloviev places the opening of the faux council on the feast day of the Exaltation of the Holy Cross. – Ed.

also members of the lower clergy and of the laity. It is seen as a tribute to progress because it has united all Christians and the representatives of the People of God.

How clever an evildoer the Antichrist can be. Nobody yet realized that he was the Antichrist. Soloviev's literary imagination highlights something which may well present difficulties for the Church in the future, namely the legitimate demand that every religious confession conserve its identity. In the past, this has led to the accusation that religion is divisive and sets men against each other. Soloviev's imaginary Council, which is not Catholic, is a Council for all religions and prefigures a proposal of uniting all religions—that may well find widespread popular acceptance—by eradicating their specific differences so as to guarantee peace.

Unmasking the Antichrist

Now we shall see how the Antichrist was discovered. The difficulty is not so much one of ascertaining the identity of his person but of grasping the spirit of seduction which he incarnates. Soloviev helps us to discover the "the great seduction" of humanitarianism, which is a religion without Christ or Cross in which man saves himself by his own intelligence. Three important characters emerge at the Council. They discover the Antichrist.

> Pope Peter II ... by right headed the Catholic part of the Council. His predecessor had died on the way to the council, and a conclave convened at Damascus unanimously elected Cardinal Simone Barionini, who took the name of Peter. He was of humble origin, from the province of Naples, and became known as a Carmelite preacher; he had done much good work in combating a certain satanic sect that had gained great influence in St. Petersburg and the

neighborhood and was leading astray both the Orthodox and the Catholics.

It fascinates me to think that Soloviev believed that the last Pope would be a Carmelite. St. Theresa of Avila, writing of the last days in her autobiography, tells that she had a vision of the religious orders who were in the front line and which had suffered martyrdom. Among them she saw the Carmelites. The last Pope, a Neapolitan, Peter II, is a man of outstanding courage, action, and intelligence. Like many Neapolitans he is not a conformist.

> He was a man of about fifty, of medium height and strong build, with a red face, an aquiline nose and bushy eyebrows. Warm-hearted and impetuous, he spoke with fervor and sweeping gestures, and carried away rather than convinced his audience. The new Pope expressed distrust and disapproval for the world-lord, especially after the late Pope, setting out for the council, had at the emperor's insistence made the imperial chancellor and the great magician, the exotic bishop Apollonius, a Cardinal. Peter considered Apollonius a dubious Catholic and an indubitable impostor.

This is an effective and positive description of great spiritual experience. His was an instinctive antipathy towards him who posed as the lord and savior of the world. He also regarded his amanuensis, Apollonius, with suspicion.

Here we encounter Soloviev's head of the Orthodox Church. He is a "starets," a highly important figure in the Russian Church who stands for the greatness of its spiritual tradition. The starets is an old man who has grown old meditating on the Word of God and praying the prayer of Christ from the heart.

The Antichrist *by Vladimir Soloviev*

The real, though unofficial, leader of the Orthodox was the Starets[13] John, very well known among the Russian people. His official status was that of a bishop "in retirement," yet he did not live in any monastery, but constantly traveled about. There were strange legends about him. Some people maintained that he was the risen Fyodor Kuzmich, that is the Emperor Alexander I, who had been born some three centuries before. Others went further and said that he was the real Starets John, i.e. the Apostle John the Divine who had never died and of late appeared openly. He himself said nothing about his origin or his youth. He was very old but still vigorous, with yellowish and even greenish white curly hair and beard, tall and thin, with full and slightly rosy cheeks, lively bright eyes and a touchingly kind expression in his face and voice; he always wore a white cassock and cloak.

Following the beautiful description of Pope Peter II and of John the starets, Soloviev introduces the head of the Protestants. Since the Protestants are great students of the Bible, their head is naturally a professor. He is one of those truly religious men who unite faith and science, faith and piety. Among the Protestants there is no shortage of such men. Dietrich Bonhoeffer (1906-1945) is a good example. He was an exemplary pastor and theologian, a man of deep faith and courage. He was martyred by the Nazis in a concentration camp. Soloviev's portrait of the professor Ernst Pauli is in many respects reminiscent of Bonhoeffer.

The leader of the Evangelical members of the council was a most learned German theologian, Professor Ernst Pauli.

[13] "Elder" in most translations. - Ed.

He was a lean old man of medium height, with a huge
forehead, sharp nose and clean-shaven chin. His eyes had
a peculiar ferociously good-natured look. He constantly
rubbed his hands, shook his head, menacingly knitted his
brows and thrust out his lips; as he did so, his eyes glittered
and he made gloomy and disjointed sounds: "so! nun! ja!
so also!" He was dressed for the occasion and wore a white
tie and a long clerical frock coat with some decorations.

The three leaders, a Catholic, an Orthodox, and a Protestant,
were men of profound faith. One was Italian, one was Russian,
and one was German. They would confront the Antichrist at the
Council.

The most famous Council in the history of mankind opens—
and, according to Soloviev, it would be the last Council. The
preparations are solemn and sumptuous. A completely lay rite is
enacted at the opening—the various confessions had their own
religious rites prior to the opening of the Council and separate from
it. The emperor, triumphant, presides at the Council, accompanied
by the Imperial Cardinal Chancellor, the magician Apollonius. As
we have already remarked, these two represent the two beasts of
chapter 13 of the book of Revelation. Their entry is greeted with
delirious applause. The emperor begins his discourse. He praises
himself; he impresses himself upon the heart of his listeners and
begins his evildoing.

> The emperor, standing by his throne and with majestic
> benignity stretching out his hand, said in a pleasant and
> sonorous voice: "Christians of all denominations! My
> beloved subjects and brothers. From the beginning of my
> reign which the Almighty has blessed with such wonder-
> ful and glorious deeds, I have not once had occasion to

be displeased with you; you have always done your duty in all faith and conscience. But this is not enough for me. My sincere love for you, my beloved brothers, longs for reciprocity. I want you, not out of a sense of duty but from heart-felt love, to recognize me as your true leader in every work undertaken for the good of humanity. And so, in addition to what I do for all, I should like to bestow special favors upon you. Christians, what can I do to make you happy? What can I give you, not as to my subjects but as to my brethren and co-believers? Christians, tell me what is most precious to you in Christianity, that I might direct my efforts to it?" He paused and waited.

He makes grandiose promises of concessions and largesse. He presumes to dispense happiness to all in exchange for total and absolute recognition of his dominion over the conscience of all mankind. In this manner, Soloviev denounces the perennial aspiration of the secular power to draw support from the Church and to manipulate it for secular purposes. The recognition of the spiritual authority of the Church by the world in exchange for secular power has always been a subtle temptation and a form of blackmail. (Be very careful when political authorities begin to praise Christianity and speak well of it.)

Christians and the Great Seduction

There was a low murmuring in the Temple. The members of the council were whispering among themselves. Pope Peter, warmly gesticulating, was explaining something to those around him. Professor Pauli was shaking his head and fiercely smacking his lips. The Starets John, bending down to an Eastern Bishop and a grey friar, was quietly admonishing them in a low voice. After waiting for a few minutes the emperor addressed the council in the same kind voice, though now there was a hardly perceptible note of irony in it: "Dear Christians," he said, "I understand how difficult it is for you to make one straightforward answer. I want to help you in this too. Unfortunately you have been broken up into various sects and parties since time immemorial and perhaps you have no longer a common aim. But if you cannot agree between yourselves I hope to bring agreement between all your parties by showing them all equal love and equal readiness to satisfy the true desire of each.

The Antichrist turns to the Catholics:

"Dear Christians! I know that for many and by no means the least of you the most precious thing is the spiritual authority which it gives to its lawful representatives—not for their own advantage, of course, but for the common good, since such authority is the basis of true spiritual order and of moral discipline which is necessary to all. Dear brother-Catholics! oh, how well I understand your view and how I should like to find support for my power in the authority of your spiritual head! That you may not regard this as mere empty talk and flattery, I solemnly declare: in accordance with my autocratic will the chief bishop of all Catholics, the Pope of Rome, is henceforth restored to his Roman see with all the rights and privileges that had ever been given it by my predecessors, beginning with the emperor Constantine the Great."

He would make them happy and return the Pope to Rome—from which he had fled—with all his sovereign prerogatives, provided that he would uphold his power. In exchange for this restoration, the Antichrist demanded his recognition as absolute lord.

> "And all I want of you, brother-Catholics, is an inner heartfelt recognition of me as your only defender and patron. Let those who regard me as such in their heart and conscience come to me here." And he pointed to the empty seats on the platform.

Dear friends, in moments such as these the Christian is distinguished by his power of discernment and by his courage. Fortunately, here we are dealing with a story. However, we must never forget that something similar happened during the Arian crisis. Here Soloviev issues a warning.

> With joyful cries "*Gratias agimus! Domine, salvum fac magnum imperatorem*" almost all the princes of the Catholic Church, cardinals and bishops, the majority of believing laymen, and more than half the monks went up on to the platform and, after low bows to the emperor, took their seats there.

This was no longer the Church. Where then, dear friends, was the Catholic Church?

> But down below, in the middle of the hall, straight and immovable as a marble statue, the Pope Peter the Second sat in his place.

The Church was to be found with the Pope. Where the Pope is, there too is the Church.

> All who had surrounded him were on the platform. But the thinned ranks of monks and laymen closed around him, forming a narrow ring, and a restrained whisper came from there: "*Non praevalebunt, non praevalebunt portae inferni.*"

This is one of the highlights of Soloviev's *Tale* because it stresses two important truths; firstly, *"ubi Petrus, ibi Ecclesia"* (where Peter is, there too is the Church) and, secondly, *"non praevalebunt"* because God has ordained that hell *shall never prevail* against the rock, who is the Pope.

The Pope avoids being manipulated. Surprised by his attitude, the emperor turns to the Orthodox with the same intent of seducing and buying them. He promises them a museum for all the great traditions to which the Orthodox are attached. He invites them to give their consent.

> "Brother-Orthodox! let those of you who appreciate my action and who whole-heartedly call me their true lord and leader, come up to me here!" A great number of hierarchs from the East and North, a half of the former Old Believers and more than half of the Orthodox priests, monks and laymen with joyful cries went up on to the platform, looking askance at the Catholics proudly seated there. But the Starets John sighed aloud and did not move. When the crowd around had considerably thinned, he left his bench and moved nearer to the Pope, Peter II, and his circle. [That is ecumenism!] He was followed by the Orthodox who had not gone up on to the platform.

The great majority has apostatized. Soloviev foretells the great apostasy and the reduction of the faithful to a tiny flock in a truly scriptural spirit.

The emperor turns to the Protestants, well knowing their sensibilities for biblical themes. The emperor says: "I know, dear Christians, that there are among you some who value most in Christianity personal conviction of truth and free inquiry into the Scriptures." He reveals that he studied the Bible in his youth. As well as being a pacifist, an ecologist, and a social reformer, he is also a great exegete. He received an honorary doctorate from the theology faculty of one of Germany's most prestigious universities. Then he tries to buy the Protestants by signing a statute:

> for the world-institute for free inquiry into the Scriptures from every possible point of view and in every possible direction, and for the study of all auxiliary subjects, with an annual budget of one and one half million marks.

He is anxious to win over the Protestants and publicly to accept their gratitude.

> "Will those of you who appreciate my attitude and can genuinely recognize me as their sovereign leader please come up here to the new doctor of theology." A strange smile twisted for a moment the great man's beautiful lips. More than half of the learned theologians moved towards the platform, though with some hesitation and delay. All looked back at Professor Pauli who seemed glued to his seat. He hunched his back, huddled himself together and hung his head. The learned theologians who had mounted the platform looked uncomfortable, and one of them, with a sudden wave of his hand, jumped straight down past the steps and ran, limping, to join Professor Pauli and the minority that had remained with him. Pauli raised his head and, getting up in an undecided sort of way, walked, followed by his staunch co-believers, past the empty benches and settled closer to the Starets John and the Pope Peter. The majority of the council had ascended onto the platform, including almost all the hierarchy of the East and West. Down below, only three groups of men remained:

one surrounded the Starets John, another Pope Peter and a third Professor Pauli.

Soloviev characterizes the great siege of the Church in terms of its protection by the civil power and of the transfer of the Church's governance to the civil authority. In return, the three Christian confessions receive a form of human security which they crave. The emperor plans to liquidate the Church and to use it to promote merely worldly enterprises. He plans to tear out the very heart of the Church: Jesus Christ crucified and risen. The great majority of Catholics (bishops and cardinals), Protestants (pastors and laity), and of the Orthodox (bishops and monks) are seduced and advance to occupy the places reserved for the apostates. Peter II, John the starets, and Professor Pauli, representatives of the three churches, remain firmly where they are, surrounded by the few remaining faithful, that tiny flock, the *pusillus grex* which remains attached to them.

At precisely this moment, they begin to realize that they have come face-to-face with the Antichrist.

The emperor is dumbfounded by the reaction of the three religious leaders and of the tiny minority still attached to them. He believes that he has offered every religious confession what they wanted.

> The emperor addressed them in a tone of sadness: "What more can I do for you? Strange men! What do you want of me? I do not know. Tell me yourselves, you Christians forsaken by most of your brothers and leaders and condemned by popular feeling: what is most precious to you in Christianity?"

Christ Is the Treasure of Christianity

The starets replies, defending the very heart of the Christian faith — its irreducible essential core:

Then, straight and slender like a white church candle, the Starets John stood up and answered gently: "Great Emperor! Most precious to us in Christianity is Christ Himself—He Himself, and everything rests on Him, for we know that in Him all the fullness of Godhead dwells bodily. But from you too, sire, we are ready to receive every blessing if only we recognize in your bountiful hand the holy hand of Christ. And here is our straight answer to your question what you can do for us: confess now here before us Jesus Christ the Son of God, who came in the flesh, rose from the dead and is coming again—confess Him, and we shall receive you with love as the true forerunner of His glorious second coming."

Dear friends, those, even in the Church, who deny that Christ is the Son of God are the precursors of the Antichrist—even when they admit that he was a great man, a great prophet, a reformer, a guru, or a thinker (cf. 1 John 2:18-19). This is the central issue. Any denial of the human and divine nature of Christ indicates a work in favor of the kingdom of the Antichrist.

He paused and looked steadily at the emperor. Something evil was happening to the great man. The same hellish storm raged within him as on that fateful night. He completely lost his inner balance, and all his thoughts were concentrated on not losing external self-control and not giving himself away too soon.

The Antichrist tries to conceal his identity. He acts as a believer and maintains a religious vocabulary. He protests his love for the Church and his obedience to its traditions and authority. However, he acts as Satan's instrument. He has dedicated himself to Satan and carries an evil project in his heart and tries to avoid having his identity revealed.

Many, at the time of his coming, will be deceived. Only those to whom the Wisdom of God has been given will be able to identify him.

> He was making superhuman efforts not to throw himself with a wild yell at the speaker and tear at him with his teeth. Suddenly he heard the familiar unearthly voice: "Be still and fear nothing." He remained silent. Only his darkened and death-like face was contorted and his eyes flashed. While the Starets John was speaking, the great magician, who sat wrapped up in a voluminous three-colored cloak that completely hid his red robe of a cardinal, seemed to be doing some manipulations under it; [he practiced magic and was in communication with Satan] there was a look of consternation in his glittering eyes, and his lips moved.

At this point, the identification of the emperor and his friend the heretic bishop Apollonius with the two beasts of Revelation becomes more than evident. We have already said that the panther is the symbol of political power. The lamb with the voice of a dragon represents religious power. Soloviev's Antichrist contains these two powers which are incarnate in the emperor and his assistant, the cardinal-magician. Both are instruments of Satan.

Benson and Soloviev regard the Antichrist as a lay politician who subjects the Church to his dominion. Other traditions do not exclude the possibility that the Antichrist will be an ecclesiastic whose power unites a religious primacy and a political craving to dominate the world.

Several writers, especially the bearers of private revelations (which, while not approved by the Church, have not been condemned), hold this view of the Antichrist. Maria Valtorta's Antichrist is an eminently religious person.

This is a matter of little consequence, for these writers are not concerned with describing *how* things will go. Some can be perplexed by these writings because they never move beyond a superficial reading of the text and become too involved with the narrative and its material details, or with the manner in which some writers imagine the Antichrist's manifestation. Benson, Soloviev, Valtorta, and others, for whose intuitions we must surely be grateful, are merely concerned to unmask the seduction of the times, that which the *Catechism of the Catholic Church* describes in article 675. Every age has its own concept of Satan and of his attempt to present a false religious message. The end will be preceded by a time of great deception. Soloviev denounces the deception of his age which took the form of a Christianity devoid of Christ.

> Through the open windows of the temple a huge black cloud could be seen gathering, and soon everything turned dark. The Starets John was still gazing with fear and amazement at the silent emperor; suddenly he drew back in horror and, turning around, cried in a stifled voice: "Children, it's the antichrist!"

Evil is in great measure conquered by its unmasking. Soloviev teaches that evil is extremely dangerous for as long as it remains undetected. When you do not realize that you have been given a spurious faith you are already in danger of spiritual disaster. When you know that you are being deceived, you have uncovered evil, which is already defeated in large part.

The real problem is to discover Satan who presents himself as an angel of light amidst the seductions of the times. Even religious seduction will deceive many, as the Gospel warns when it speaks of false prophets (Matt. 24:11). Soloviev's *Tale* concludes with a simple proverb: All that glistens is not gold.

At the moment when the starets, inspired by the Wisdom of God, exposes the Antichrist, Apollonius unleashes his Satanic magic and performs false prodigies to "deceive many."

> At that moment there was a deafening crash of thunder, a huge ball of lightning flared up in the temple and enveloped the starets. All were stock-still for a moment. When the Christians recovered from the shock, the Starets John was dead. The emperor, pale but calm, addressed the assembly: "You have seen God's judgment. I did not wish for any one's death, but my heavenly father avenges his beloved son. The case is settled. Who would dare to oppose the Almighty? Secretaries! write: The ecumenical council of all Christians, when the fire from heaven had struck the insane opponent of the divine majesty, unanimously recognized the mighty emperor of Rome and world as their supreme leader and lord."

The Antichrist portrays the death of John the starets as a divine approval for himself and claims to be the Almighty's beloved Son and his representative who has been invested with sovereignty over Christians.

Contradicitur

He underestimated Peter II, the fierce Neapolitan:

> Suddenly a word spoken loudly and clearly resounded through the temple: "*contradicitur*." Pope Peter II, purple in the face and shaking with anger, stood up and raised his staff in the emperor's direction. "Our only Lord is Jesus

Christ, the Son of the living God. And what you are—you
have just heard. Begone from us, you Cain! Begone you
vessel of the devil! By the power of Christ, I, the servant
of the servants of God, forever expel you, a vile dog, from
God's fold and deliver you to your father, Satan! Anathema,
anathema, anathema."

The Pope Excommunicates the Lord of the World

Who would dare to have addressed a victor celebrating his triumph?
This is confession of the faith, even to the point of death. One
can die for the faith. One must die for the faith.

> While he was speaking the great magician restlessly moved
> under his cloak; there was a clap of thunder louder than
> the last anathema, and the last Pope fell down dead. "This
> is how all my enemies shall perish at my father's hand," said
> the emperor. "*Pereant, pereant*," cried the trembling princes
> of the Church [who had apostatized]. He turned and, lean-
> ing on the shoulder of the great magician, slowly walked
> out of the door at the back of the platform, followed by all
> his crowd. There were left in the hall two corpses and a
> throng of Christians half-dead with fear.

Behold the Church reduced to two corpses and a tiny group of
Christians drawn from among Catholics, Protestants, and the
Orthodox.

> Professor Pauli, head of the believing and fervent Protes-
> tants, bore courageous witness.
> The general terror seemed to have roused all the pow-
> ers of his spirit. His very appearance changed—he looked
> inspired and majestic. With resolute steps he mounted the

platform and sitting down in the empty seat of one of the secretaries of state took up a piece of paper and began writing. When he had finished, he stood up and read aloud: "To the glory of our only Savior, Jesus Christ. From the ecumenical council of God's churches, gathered in Jerusalem: after our most blessed brother John, the representative of Eastern Christianity, had denounced the great deceiver and enemy of God as antichrist, foretold in Holy Writ, and our most blessed father Peter, the representative of Western Christianity, rightfully and lawfully excommunicated him for life, the council in the presence of the bodies of these two witnesses of Christ killed for the truth, has decided: cease all intercourse with the excommunicated and his vile conclave, and, withdrawing to the wilderness, await the impending coming of our true Lord, Jesus Christ."

This is an amazing linguistic coincidence. Soloviev refers to his Antichrist as the "great impostor" while the *Catechism of the Catholic Church* refers to the greatest deception as being that of the Antichrist (675).

The crowd [the little flock] was filled with animation. There were loud cries of "*Adveniat! Adveniat cito!* [Come, come quickly!] *Komm, Herr Jesu, komm!* [one of Johann Sebastian Bach's most beautiful motets] Come, Lord Jesus."

The faith, dear friends, is the power that overcomes the world. Those who have the faith are true victors. The others, however, are destined for eternal damnation.

Professor Pauli made a postscript and read: "Having unanimously adopted this first and last act of the last ecumenical council, we append our signatures thereto" — and he made a gesture of invitation to the assembly. All hastily mounted the platform and signed. The last to sign, in large Gothic script, was "*duorum defunctorum testium locum tenens Ernst Pauli.*" [Ernst Pauli, locum tenens for two deceased witnesses.]

Here we must refer to Revelation and its two witnesses who confess the faith during the great persecution. They were killed but rose again (Rev. 11:11). Soloviev reads the passage literally.

"Now let us go with our tabernacle of the last testament!" he said, pointing to the two dead men. The bodies were put on stretchers. To the singing of Latin, German, and Church-Slavonic hymns the Christians slowly walked to the exit from Haram-ash-Sharif. There the procession was stopped by the secretary of state, sent by the emperor and accompanied by an officer with a platoon of the guards. The soldiers stopped by the door, and the secretary read aloud: "The order of his divine Majesty: to instill reason into the Christian people and protect them from evil-minded men who cause trouble and sedition, we have thought fit to exhibit the bodies of the two mischief-makers, killed by fire from heaven, in the street of the Christians (Haret-en-Nasara) at the entrance to their chief temple, called the temple of the Sepulchre and also of the Resurrection, so that all may convince themselves of their actual death. As to the partisans who maliciously reject all our benefactions and foolishly shut their eyes to obvious manifestations of the Deity, through our mercy and intercession with the heavenly Father they are spared death by heavenly fire which they deserve and are left entirely free except for the prohibition, for the sake of the common good, to dwell in cities and other populated places lest they disturb and offend the innocent and simple-minded people by their evil inventions." When they had finished reading, eight soldiers, at a sign from the officer, approached the stretchers on which the bodies were laid.

The emperor resorts to the tactic of persuasion. He exposes both corpses that all may see the justice of God, while he leaves the other Christians at liberty. The last Christians, together with Professor Pauli, take refuge in Jericho. They believe that the end of the world has come, for the Antichrist has been made manifest.

In Jerusalem, the emperor, standing before the apostate members of the Council who had flocked to him, orders the representatives of the Catholic hierarchy immediately to proceed, by abbreviated process, to the election of a worthy successor for the Apostle Peter.

> The presence of the emperor as the leader and representative of Christendom would more than make up for omissions in the ritual, and ... in the name of all Christians, he suggested that the Sacred College should elect his beloved friend and brother Apollonius, so that the intimate bond between them would make the union between the Church and the state secure and indissoluble, to the benefit of both. The Sacred College withdrew to a special room for the conclave and in an hour and a half returned with the new Pope Apollonius.

Clearly, a Sacred College formed of apostates, and presided over by an excommunicate, lacks the moral characteristics required by the faith to elect a Pope. The apostate cardinal-bishop, an adept of magic, is eventually elected by a Sacred College which has defected from the faith. He is a false pope and his election is null and void.

Here we are in the realm of the imagination, but Soloviev's tale contains many useful lessons. Satan, at the time of the great deception, will try to deceive even the faithful—if that were possible, as Scripture says—by falsification. The details of the Antichrist's appearance well demonstrate the cunning of the great deception which will lead the impure of heart into error.

> While the election was being held the emperor was gently, wisely and eloquently persuading the Orthodox and Evangelical delegates to end their old dissensions in view of the new great era in Christian history; he pledged his word that Apollonius would know how to do away forever with all the historical abuses of the papacy.

The Antichrist unites Catholics, Orthodox, and Protestants. He presents them with a pope who is completely subjected to his dominion for the common good of humanity. This is truly a great deception.

> The Orthodox and Protestant delegates, convinced by his speech, drew up an act of union between the churches, and when, amidst joyful acclamations, Apollonius appeared on the platform with the cardinals, a Greek archbishop and an Evangelical minister presented their paper to him. "*Accipio et approbo et laetificatur cor meum,*" said Apollonius, signing the document, "I am a true Orthodox and a true Protestant as much as I am a true Catholic," he added and exchanged friendly kisses with the Greek and the German. Then he walked up to the emperor, who put his arms around him and held him in his embrace for some minutes.

The Wrath of God

The new pope, the Antipope, approves and assents to the union of the churches. Soloviev foresees in this a certain type of ecumenism which is a false ecumenism.

The Reign of Satan

The reign of Satan begins. Soloviev describes the spectacles which are used for deception and seduction.

> Meanwhile curious points of light flittered in all directions about the palace and the temple; they grew and transformed themselves into luminous forms of strange beings; flowers never seen on earth before fell in showers from above, filling the air with a mysterious fragrance. Delightful heart-melting sounds of strange musical instruments floated from on high, and angelic voices of invisible singers glorified the new lords of heaven and earth.

Spine-chilling things begin to happen. The souls of the damned in Hell come to know of Satan's rule on earth and clamor to be set free.

> In the meantime a terrible subterranean roar was heard in the northwestern corner of the central palace under *kubbet-el-aruah*, i.e., the cupola of souls, where, according to the Moslem tradition, lies the entrance into Hades. When, at the emperor's invitation, the assembly moved in that direction, all clearly heard innumerable high-pitched and piercing voices—children's or devils'—calling out: "The time has come, release us, saviors, saviors, saviors!" But when Apollonius, pressing himself close to the wall, thrice shouted something to those under the earth in an unknown tongue, the voices were still and the subterranean

roar subsided. While all this was going on, an immense crowd of people surrounded Haram-ash-Sharif. When it grew dark, the emperor, together with the new pope, came out on the eastern balcony, raising "a storm of enthusiasm." He graciously bowed in all directions, while Apollonius continually took from large baskets, brought to him by cardinal-deacons, and threw into the air magnificent Roman candles, rockets and fiery sprays, pearly-phosphorescent or bright rainbow-colored, that caught fire at the touch of his hand. On reaching the ground they all turned into innumerable different-colored sheets of paper with complete and unconditional indulgences for all sins, past, present and future.

Satan doubles his extraordinary feats which quickly become surrogates for signs of divine favor. A new and false religious authority is established—that of the lamb with the voice of the dragon. At this point, Soloviev's *Tale* takes a purely fantastic turn, without, however, failing in its purpose of instruction. It describes the reign of Satan as a great religious deception which will seduce many.

Popular rejoicing surpassed all bounds. True, some people said that they had seen with their own eyes the indulgences turn into hideous toads and snakes; but an overwhelming majority were enthusiastic. Public festivities went on for a few more days, and the new miracle-working pope performed things so wonderful and incredible that it would be quite useless to describe them.

Soloviev's false religion is a religion with a false Christ and a false Church. But where is the true Church and the true Christ?

The Wrath of God

Where Is the True Church and the True Christ?

During this time the Christians on the desert heights of Jericho devoted themselves to fasting and prayer. On the evening of the fourth day, after dark, Professor Pauli and nine companions made their way to Jerusalem with asses and a cart, and went by the side streets to Haret-en-Nasara, approaching the entrance to the temple of the Resurrection, where the bodies of Pope Peter II and the Starets John lay on the pavement. The streets were deserted at that hour, for the whole town had gone to Haram-ash-Sharif. The sentries on duty were fast asleep. The rescue party found that the bodies were untouched by corruption and had not even grown stiff or heavy. Putting them on the stretchers and covering them with cloaks brought for the purpose, the party returned by the same circuitous way to their people. As soon as they put the stretchers on the ground, the spirit of life returned to the dead. They stirred, trying to throw off the cloaks that covered them. With joyful cries all rushed to help them and soon both the risen men were on their feet, safe and sound.

These are the two witnesses of Revelation who return to life (Rev. 11:11).

The true union of Christians will come about at the time of persecution when the flock will be reduced to a minimum.

> And having come to life, the Starets John said: "Well, my dear children, so we are not parted after all. And this is what I tell you now: it is time that we fulfilled Christ's prayer about His disciples that they should be one, as He and the Father are one. For the sake of this unity in Christ, my children, let us honor our beloved brother Peter. Let him pasture Christ's sheep to the last. There, brother!" —and he embraced Peter. Professor Pauli came

up to them. "*Tu es Petrus!*" said he to the Pope. "*Jetz ist es ja gründlich erwiesen und ausser jedem Zweifel gesetzt.*"[14] And he warmly pressed Peter's hand with his right hand and gave his left to John, saying: "*So also, Väterchen, nun sind wir ja Eins in Christo.*"[15] This was how the union of the Churches took place on a dark night, in a high and solitary place. But night's darkness was suddenly lit up with a bright light, a great sign appeared in the sky: a woman clothed with the sun, and the moon under her feet, and upon her head a crown of twelve stars. The sign remained in the same spot for some time, and then slowly moved southwards. Pope Peter raised his staff and cried: "This is our banner! Let us follow it!" And he walked in the direction of the vision, followed by both the elders and the whole crowd of Christians—towards God's Mount, Sinai.

At this point, Soloviev uses a literary device to conclude his *Tale*. The *Tale* is really an old manuscript which has been rediscovered. It had been written by an Orthodox starets, Pansophius, who, having reached this point in the story, was unable to finish it. In conversation with a friend, he merely outlined the conclusion before his death. The epilogue reads:

When the spiritual leaders and representatives of Christianity retired to the Arabian desert, where crowds of the faithful devotees of the truth flocked to them from all countries of the world, the new pope was able without hindrance to demoralize with his miracles all the other, superficial Christians, not disillusioned about the

---

[14] "Now this is thoroughly proved and established beyond all doubt."
[15] "So now, Little Father, we are really one in Christ."

antichrist. He declared that by the power of his keys he had opened the doors between the earthly world and the world beyond the grave, and indeed intercourse between the dead and the living, and also between men and demons, became a thing of everyday occurrence, and there developed new and unheard-of kinds of mystical fornication and idolatry.

It is extraordinary that a book such as this, written a century ago, should have been able to predict the rise of various satanic cults as well as the search for contact with the dead which have become mass phenomena. Soloviev read the signs of the times with great intuition and clearly foresaw the development of certain tendencies as though he were a seer. Undoubtedly he was able to do this because of his notable spiritual intelligence.

The Unexpected

The emperor began to consider himself firmly established on the religious ground, and at the insistent suggestion of the secret father's voice declared himself to be the only true incarnation of the supreme Deity; but at this point he was faced with a new trouble from an utterly unexpected quarter: the Jews rose up against him.

In his Letter to the Romans, St. Paul repeatedly says that the time will come when the great monotheist religion will be roused to definitive witness of the truth (cf. *Catechism of the Catholic Church*, 674).

This nation, at the time numbering some thirty millions, had a share in preparing and consolidating the superman's world-wide success. And when he moved to Jerusalem, secretly encouraging the Jewish rumors that his main purpose was to establish Israel's world domination, the Jews acknowledged him as Messiah, and their enthusiastic devotion to him knew no bounds. But suddenly they rebelled, breathing anger and vengeance. This sudden change, no doubt predicted both by the Scriptures and tradition, was explained by Fr. Pansophius perhaps rather too simply and realistically. The fact was that the Jews, who regarded the emperor as a full-blooded and perfect Israelite, accidentally discovered that he had not even been circumcised. On that very day the whole of Jerusalem and on the next day the whole of Palestine were in revolt. Boundless and ardent devotion to the savior of Israel, the promised messiah, was replaced by hatred, as boundless and as ardent, for the perfidious deceiver, the impudent impostor. The whole of Jewry rose up as one man, and its enemies saw with surprise that in its real depths the soul of Israel lived not by calculations and greed for gain, but by the power of heartfelt emotion—by the hope and wrath of its centuries-old messianic faith. The emperor, who had not expected such a sudden outburst, lost his self-control and issued an edict sentencing to death all rebellious Jews and Christians. Many thousands and tens of thousands who had not time to arm were slaughtered without mercy. But soon a million-strong army of Jews gained possession of Jerusalem and surrounded the antichrist in Haram-ash-Sharif. He had at his disposal only part of the guards and could not cope with the massed enemy. With the help of his Pope's magical arts the emperor succeeded in making his way through the besiegers' ranks, and soon appeared in Syria with an innumerable army of different heathen tribes. The Jews set out to meet him with small hope of success.

But just as the advance guard of both armies were about to meet there was an earthquake of unheard-of violence: under the Dead Sea, in the vicinity of which the emperor's troops were encamped, a huge volcano burst open and rivers of fire, merging into one flaming lake, swallowed up the emperor with all his numberless regiments and his inseparable companion Pope Apollonius, whose magic proved of no avail.

Dear friends, when God calls a halt to something, it is a halt, and no magic can stop Him.

The Jews ran toward Jerusalem in fear and trembling, calling on the God of Israel to save them. As they came in sight of the holy city, the sky was rent in two by a great lightning reaching from east to west, and they saw Christ coming down from Heaven in royal array with wounds from the nails in His outstretched hands. At the same time a crowd of Christians led by Peter, John and Paul, was approaching Sion from Sinai, and from all sides other enthusiastic crowds were running: those were the Jews and Christians executed by the antichrist. They came to life again and reigned with Christ for a thousand years. Fr. Pansophius intended to conclude his tale in this way. Its subject was not the catastrophic end of the world, but the conclusion of an historical evolution: the manifestation, triumph and defeat of the antichrist.

Soloviev gives a literal interpretation to Revelation 20:2–6, which speaks of the kingdom which will endure for a thousand years. However, this passage must be understood in a spiritual sense. The appearance of Christ on earth to institute a reign which will last for a thousand years prior to the end of the world and the final defeat of Satan, must be interpreted as the reign of Christ in our hearts and the civilization of love to which Paul VI refers.

Soloviev does not situate the coming of the Antichrist at the end of the world. He regards his appearance as the penultimate assault of the Evil One, after which a reign of a thousand years will follow. Then will come Satan's final assault and the end of the world.

Maria Valtorta shares Soloviev's vision of the end of the world. Other writers, including Benson, regard the fall of the Antichrist, the end of the world, and the judgment as simultaneous events. The biblical text, therefore, is subject to varying interpretations. For St. Paul, however, the reign of the Antichrist and the end of the world are closely linked. This view is also taken by the *Catechism of the Catholic Church* and seems preferable to me.

These details are of less interest for us. The interpretation of prophecies is prone to human error and confusion. The first Christians believed that Christ was on the point of return at any moment. We should be careful to avoid the error of believing that prophecies contain specific times for what will happen in the future or signs indicating when these things will take place.

The writings of Soloviev, Benson, Valtorta, and others are valuable works not because they anticipate events in the future, but because of their power to analyze and unmask the errors of our own age. They also denounce every attempt to falsify the true faith. Seen in this light, such literary works can be very useful, especially for our understanding of the times in which we live.

Today, for instance, the realization that the Catholic faith is the true faith can easily be lost. Attempts to create a universal religion by fusing all religions can be very convincing. It is easy to succumb to the temptation of modernizing Catholicism by denuding it of its essentials: Christ and His Cross. In circumstances such as these, Soloviev, Benson, Valtorta, and others can be usefully read by the faithful. Valtorta particularly emphasizes the religious deceptions of the Antichrist's reign.

I shall conclude our reading of Soloviev's *Tale* by quoting its closing lines. A reader asks: "What is the real meaning of this drama? I do not understand: Why does the Antichrist hate God so much, since he is basically good, and not bad?" The reply: "The fact is that 'basically' he is not good. This is the whole point of the tale. The Antichrist can be summarized by the proverb: 'All that glitters is not gold.' The splendor of something counterfeit has no real authentic force."

The *Tale* sets out to remind us of St. Paul's warning to be on our guard against Satan (2 Cor. 13-15) when he comes as the Angel of Light, presenting a false Christ and a false Church. He presents them as something attractive and modern but, in reality, they tear the very heart out of Christianity.

Conclusion

Dear friends, we are approaching a time of trial when the precious gift of the faith will be put to the test. Many are losing the faith, but this is not the only problem which we are facing.

Loss of faith and turning one's back on Christ are grave and sad events. Today, however, the faith is put to another test which is no less difficult. That test is one of adhering to a false faith. Subjectivism is widespread in contemporary culture. It can reduce the Christian faith to a few selected truths coupled with other elements borrowed from different religions. All religions are portrayed as equally valid ways to salvation. Indeed, there is an effort to create a kind of religious "supermarket." In this climate, even Catholics, instead of believing that the Catholic Church is the one true Church, are inclined to be selective about truths from the religious "supermarket." Some choose only those truths which are convenient and comfortable. Subjective selection of religious truths is just another means of inducing spiritual shipwreck.

The faith can also be lost by a third and more subtle manner. Within the Church—as Paul VI said—a non-Christian thought is abroad. It consists in presenting a false Church which is not Christ's Church, and a false Christ who is not the Son of God. These tendencies can seduce many Catholics and cause them to lose the faith.

At the end of our journey, we can only come to the conclusion that these are times for vigilance, prayer, fidelity, attachment to Christ, the Gospel, the Cross, Our Lady, and the Pope, who is the rock on whom Christ built His Church. With these certainties to guide us and with a pure heart, we can survive these difficult times for the Church and for ourselves without running aground.

May the Lord grant to us who live at the end of this century to be able to say with St. Paul in 2 Timothy 4:7, "I have fought the good fight to the end; I have run the race to the finish; I have kept the faith;" Catholic, Apostolic, and Roman.

Lord of the World by Robert Hugh Benson

Introduction

Following our presentation of Soloviev's famous *Tale of the Antichrist*, we now move to another book devoted to the same theme, which belongs to a peculiar literary genre: the theologico-apocalyptic novel of Robert Hugh Benson. It has a serious theme: the coming of the Antichrist. The Antichrist is cited not only in novels but also in the Bible. He should be approached seriously: we have to remember that we are dealing with the future. The Lord, to whom the future belongs, admonishes us to "watch" and attentively study the signs of the times. This should be done in serenity and without the kind of preoccupations of past times — especially those evident at the end of the first millennium and at the beginning of the second millennium when some special significant event was widely expected.

From the many reasons which would recommend our choice of theme, perhaps the most compelling is the fact that we do not often move from one millennium to another. The second millennium is drawing to a close. In a very short while we shall arrive at the year 2000. Not every generation, dear friends, has been as fortunate — or unfortunate — as ours in seeing the passing of one millennium and the advent of another.

The Wrath of God

Will There Be a Third Millennium?

Dear friends, will there be a third millennium? If there will, what kind of millennium will it be?

These are spontaneous questions that spring from the heart. In the past few decades they have given rise to a certain submerged—or half-hidden—reading of events based on private revelations, all too frequently unworthy of any form of educated consideration. However, they do feed gossip and the reflection of many popular prayer groups.

Perhaps theologians who specialize in scientific work, or bishops who are preoccupied with preaching the Word of God and promoting sound doctrine, will be somewhat surprised to learn of some of the things stirring in the undergrowth of the forest. I can assure you that the Catholic undergrowth is teeming with so-called "private revelations" concerning the year 2000, the second coming of Christ and the appearance of the Antichrist. Indeed, some of these revelations, already widely accepted, even by some of the clergy, speak of the Antichrist's coming in a very short time. In view of the Pope's conviction that we are facing a third millennium of toil to ensure the preaching of the Gospel, I have been bold enough to declare on radio that I do not believe that we are close to the end of the world and to the Lord's coming. Letters of protest, even from priests, pour in to me announcing the imminent arrival of the Antichrist.

Experiencing the wane of one millennium and the dawn of another is certainly not an insignificant event. We shall take up the gauntlet in response to Cardinal Biffi's challenge at the Rimini Meeting of 1992. Following his initiative, we shall delve into the theme of the Antichrist.

Robert Benson

After Soloviev's magnificent little book, written almost a century ago, we now move to another writer. Unlike Soloviev, he is not

Orthodox, but an English Catholic and a convert from Anglicanism. Robert Hugh Benson, son of E. W. Benson (1829–1896), Anglican Archbishop of Canterbury, was born at Wellington College in 1871 and died at Salford in 1914. His spiritual odyssey led to a decisive reading of Newman's[16] works and culminated with his conversion to Catholicism. Ordained a priest, he devoted his ministry, which coincided with most of the mature period of his short life, to preaching and writing. Among the significant themes of his preaching, that of intimate friendship with the Lord is most important. The splendid sermons preached by Benson on this subject have been collected and published by Jaca Books as *L'Amicizia di Cristo* (Milan, 1989). This collection well illustrates the advanced levels to which Benson had progressed in the mystical life. As far as his literary acumen is concerned, Benson secured fame—and enduring fame at that because of its prophetic quality—with the publication of his novel *The Lord of the World*, which has also been reissued by Jaca as *Il Padrone del mondo* (Milan, 1997).

Lord of the World and Tale of the Antichrist

Although very different in form, Benson's novel is not in the least inferior to Soloviev's book. While both have many themes in common, Soloviev's objectives are ecclesial while Benson's are social and political. We have already posed the question of the Antichrist and, while it is not of immediate interest to us, we can legitimately ask: "Who will be the Antichrist?"

Scripture has nothing specific to say on this point. St. Paul calls him the man of iniquity (2 Thess. 2:3). But who is the "man

---

[16] John Henry Newman (1801–1890), English convert to the faith, created cardinal by Leo XIII in 1879, began a movement of conversion—or return—to Catholicism.

of iniquity"? Is he another Judas or clerical traitor or a religious leader? Could he be a layman or even a politician?

The prophetic imagination of Soloviev and Benson describe the Antichrist as a layman. Soloviev, as we have seen, associates the Antichrist, who is a politician obsessed by religion, with a kind of magician—the apostate bishop, Apollonius, who is server at the altar of power. Benson also sees the Antichrist as a politician. He is an American layman who introduces himself as lord of the world, in whose gift it is to grant universal peace, progress, and brotherly concord to all nations. It is fascinating to observe that both Soloviev and Benson present their characters in a positive light. While the Bible describes the Antichrist as the man of iniquity, Soloviev's and Benson's literary characters are not imposed by force of arms. Rather, they are sustained by popular and universal consent. They enjoy the adulation of the press, the support of other powerful figures and of the people. The Antichrist is the most popular man ever seen on the face of the earth.

It is easy to see that he is the antithesis of Christ: Christ was eliminated, crucified, killed in shame and condemned as a criminal. The Antichrist, the reverse image of Christ, becomes lord of the world by popular consent: he will be proclaimed a god, supreme lord, and supreme savior. His universal dominion is based on popular acclaim.

At one level, Soloviev and Benson are agreed: the Antichrist is seen as a positive person in worldly terms; he brings peace and progress. He persuades man that God does not exist apart from man himself. He convinces them that he himself, the Antichrist, is the first manifestation of God. According to Benson, he is a perfectly calm, cool, fascinating, and multilingual man. He is the man of peace, destiny, and providence. The world acknowledges him as king, lord, and emperor. Hatred of Christ is the one essential trait common to the Antichrist as portrayed by Soloviev and Benson.

Here I should like to contrast both writers to highlight their profound differences. The enemy of the Antichrist for Soloviev is the very person of Christ. For Catholic Benson, it is the Catholic Church. Soloviev has his Antichrist deny Christ by screaming: "He is not risen! He is rotten! He is rotten in the tomb!" Benson's Antichrist methodically, obstinately, perfectly premeditates the destruction of the Catholic Church, which is seen as the source of every evil and heresy and the plague of humanity: Felsenburgh's motto reads: *"Ecclesia Catholica delenda est!"* (The Catholic Church must be destroyed.) To me, this seems much more relevant, even if Soloviev's acute intuition succeeds in focusing on the contemporary widespread intolerance of the unity of Christ in an attempt—as Cardinal Biffi believes—to destroy the person of Christ as Son of God and to present Christianity merely as a system of humanitarian values.

Benson, on the other hand, and this is a most interesting aspect of his vision, emphasizes the world's, and the spirit of the world's, desire to destroy the Catholic Church because it is the only true witness for the supernatural.

Perhaps these two traits which characterize the Antichrist in a prophetic way should be taken together: today we witness an intolerance for Christ who is, so to speak, "degraded" by the negation of His divinity and of His unity. He is presented only as a man—although one of the greatest that ever has been. At the same time, the enemy to be destroyed today (and let us admit it) is the Catholic Church.

I should also like to highlight another contrast between Soloviev and Benson. Both writers envisage the Antichrist as a layman, a politician, in effect as a man of power. It is, however, interesting to note that while Benson situates the Antichrist at the end of the world, whose supreme manifestation will coincide with the coming of Christ at the end of history, Soloviev sees the arrival of the Antichrist at the close of one historical period, after which follows a period of enlightenment, in which Christ will dwell with men and live for a thousand years. It would appear that both writers are inspired by different traditions. One tradition situates the Antichrist at the end of the world, while the other looks forward to a period of peace and intimacy with God (the reign of a thousand years) for those who suffer the final trial at the time of the appearance of the Antichrist.

Benson's view is based on St. Paul's Second Epistle to the Thessalonians and on a correct interpretation of St. John's Revelation according to which the appearance of the Antichrist coincides with the Final Judgment and the end of human history. This tradition envisages no kingdom of a thousand years. Naturally, it is an open question for exegesis to discover if John and Paul intended to place the appearance of the Antichrist at the end of the world. Will the Antichrist come at the end of the world? John and Paul would seem to reply in the affirmative.

Soloviev's view is based on chapter twenty of the Revelation to St. John, which, when taken literally, lends itself to the interpretation that the Antichrist's appearance will be followed by a kingdom of a thousand years. This interpretation has been constantly repudiated by the Church (CCC 676).

I regard Benson as a more complex writer than Soloviev. His novel is more complete and, in a certain sense, more modern. While the main protagonist in Soloviev's work is the Antichrist in person, that of Benson's is the opposition of two realities: one part, the larger and more populous, consisting of humanity or what Benson calls "the humanitarians," who assert that nothing exists which is superior to man, and who regard man as God. The smaller part of humanity consists of "supernaturalists" and is identified with a small group of Catholics who affirm the existence of God who is distinct from man and assert the divinity of Christ. According to Benson, all religions, with the exception of Catholicism, will be absorbed by humanitarianism. Hence this important difference must be borne in mind: in Soloviev the figure of the Antichrist is preponderant while in Benson that preponderance is represented by the "spirit of the world" and the Antichrist is merely its "epiphany." The spirit of the world, which is, practically speaking, a world which has lost the faith and deifies man, is determined to eradicate Christianity by destroying all Catholics and by obliging mankind to profess belief in absolute atheism—what a tremendous project! Here, dear friends, we are not talking of mere fables but of something which lurks in the consciousness of our times.

As anticipated, the publication of *Lord of the World* in 1907 provoked an animated debate, often marked by polemics. The main themes of the novel, however, remain valid even today. Its interest is not to be found in its prediction of the Antichrist or in its description of his character. Ninety years later, its relevance consists in its having anticipated many of the characteristics of our ever more atheistic society with its apostasy and its introspective gazing on man who has increasingly become a kind of demiurge. It is also increasingly convinced that man's salvation can be entrusted to man himself. Benson describes a more advanced society where life has become more convenient because of scientific progress and the advance of technology. Man's eternal problems, including death, seem to have been resolved. In this society, the multitudes have been imbued with a rampant (and myopic) belief in the triumph of man and are inspired by the powerful. It has eradicated, or at least tried to eradicate, every aspiration of the mind toward the mystery of God. In Catholicism, that witness for the supernatural which must be denied, it has identified an insuperable obstacle for the religion of man. Benson's protagonists are Julian Felsenburgh, the Antichrist, who, in his power and endless worldly success, represents the spirit and victory of humanitarianism. Fr. Percy Franklin becomes the last Pope and takes the name Silvester. He incorporates the resistance of the Church at the end times and its struggle for the trophy of the faith. Besides these, other characters give expression to the dilettante's fascination with the plan to make man supreme lord, in contrast with his life and nature. There are those who betray the faith and, in full consciousness, abandon themselves to the seduction in all its vileness. There are those who fully agree with the new ideals and cooperate enthusiastically in their realization. There are those who fully accept humanitarianism but are filled with intolerable doubts when power shows its ferociousness and the abject things of which it is capable.

Apart from the imaginative outline, Benson's novel is alarming in a way that cannot be ignored. It grapples with the temptation to restrict human existence to an earthly horizon and to eliminate from it, not only every supernatural prospect, but also the foundation of all authentic liberty. So, too, with the blind presumption of manipulating human existence as an object of personal pleasure. In our times, such perspectives have become realities and are no longer mere conjectures.

Before proceeding to read, or better, to explore Benson's novel, I should like to reflect on some general problems that will help us better to understand our reflections.

The "End Times" in Contemporary Beliefs and Literature

Here, I should like to present a general view of the flourishing literature and beliefs about the Antichrist which proliferate as the end of the millennium approaches. Our overview will be guided by the objective and sure standpoint afforded by right doctrine as presented in Sacred Scripture and in the *Catechism of the Catholic Church*. This will enable us to evaluate correctly the various prophecies. For the necessary biblical and theological framework of this endeavor, I would refer you to the introduction to Soloviev's book.

While Benson and Soloviev certainly can be counted as great writers, we should not forget that there have been other accounts of the existence of the Antichrist in this century. These have situated his manifestation in very different terms. Some works are problematic and have rarely come to the notice of public opinion or discussion. Where this has happened, it can be explained in terms of the literary merit of such works.

The selection before us is vast and, hence, we have to limit ourselves to a few works which we have chosen because they appear credible—at least from a literary perspective—and because of the popular success that these have enjoyed.

Maria Valtorta is certainly one of those writers who enjoys a continuous and persistent literary success. She is the author not only of the famous *Vita di Gesù*, recently republished under the title *L'Evangelo come mi è stato rivelato* and in English under the title *The Poem of the Man-God*, but also of several other works claiming to contain private revelations. These latter have been collected into *Quaderni*. Of particular note are those for the years 1943, 1944, and 1945.

As is often the case when dealing with private revelations, Maria Valtorta was a controversial figure and a much-discussed writer. Here, we shall set aside the question of whether or not her writings constitute private revelations and interest ourselves in her writings merely as literary phenomena. Her books have been enormously successful. Although Maria Valtorta wrote her

Quaderni almost fifty years ago, they continue to be as popular as ever. Time is always a good judge.

At the outset, I must say that I have always esteemed Maria Valtorta. Her life of Jesus has merits as a source of edification for the faithful and has been helpful for the simple faithful in conserving the faith. *The Poem of the Man-God* has been enormously successful and has been translated into ten languages.[17] I am convinced that Valtorta knew the hearts of the simple people. She lived the plain, though contested, truth that Jesus really existed and that the Gospel is truly the Gospel of Jesus Christ. I believe that the reassertion of the historical character of Jesus and of the Gospel is Maria Valtorta's greatest contribution to strengthening the faith of ordinary people.

Of notable importance are the *Quaderni* for 1943 and 1945 when Maria Valtorta was an evacuee. She states that these writings were "dictated" to her by Jesus. Few realize that her writings contain some stupendous pages about the Antichrist. I mention them because Valtorta introduces a new strand, which differs from Benson and Soloviev. Her writings are of interest also for what she has to say about the Antichrist and the time of his appearance.

We have seen how Benson and Soloviev regard the Antichrist as a politician who turns political power, man's own power, into an absolute object of adoration and worship. As we have seen, both authors belong to the great tradition of Revelation, Maccabees, the book of Daniel, and the other biblical books which repudiate the substitution and adoration of political power instead of God.

Maria Valtorta wrote during the era of Hitler, the SS, and Stalin. According to what she says Jesus told her, she sees these

---

[17] This is not to be construed as our endorsement. The Vatican has disapproved of *The Poem of the Man-God.* —Publisher.

figures as precursors of the Antichrist. Their task is to create the conditions which lead to the degeneration and perversion of the human race. These conditions bring to life what she describes. Here something new emerges which is of great cultural interest and which we should all bear in mind. (We have the right to know the opinions of others, but the facts will determine who is right and who is wrong.) Maria Valtorta maintains that the Antichrist is not a lay politician but a man in religion. He is not a persecutor, born outside the Church. He is someone born in the Church but who betrays the Church. Like Judas, he desires to take the place of Christ. It is a less well known but nevertheless disturbing theory that Judas desired to take the place of Christ. What is highly original in Maria Valtorta's writings is her identification of the Antichrist with a man of religion, indeed with a prince of the Church, with one who was a star in the ecclesiastical firmament. He had reached the heights of the spiritual life but was seduced by Satan. He betrayed the Church and by his own perversion he attempted to pervert the entire Church. This description of the Antichrist differs completely from those of Benson and Soloviev.

Let us read from the famous *Quaderni* written in 1943 (Centro Editoriale Valtortiano). While receiving her "dictations," Maria Valtorta had asked Jesus about the Antichrist and who he might be. (I emphasize that the answers to these questions are those of Valtorta, who says that they were dictated to her by Jesus, and I make no judgment about them, as I am interested in them only as text.)

> What you are experiencing [in 1943] are only the precursors of him whom I have allowed to bear the name of negation, evil made flesh, horrors, sacrilege, Son of Satan, vendetta, destruction.... I could continue to attribute other names

of clear and frightening meaning to him. But he has not
yet come.

The various Hitlers and Stalins who dominated the world in 1943
are but the precursors of him who will be called by these names
which designate the Antichrist. But who exactly is the Antichrist?
Valtorta writes:

> He will be a highly exalted person—as exalted as the stars.
> He will not be a human star shining in a human firmament,
> but a star from a supernatural sphere which, in bowing to
> the praises of Satan, the enemy, who will know pride after
> humility, atheism after faith, immodesty after chastity, the
> fame of gold after the poverty of the Gospel, the thirst for
> honors after self-effacement.

Hence, he is an important ecclesiastic, a star of the Church. Naturally, and let it be clearly stated, this person could never be the
Pope, because the Pope is the Vicar of Christ and cannot be the
Antichrist. This is not a lot of information but it is certain. Thus
the Antichrist will be a man of great ecclesiastical prestige who has
already reached great heights in the spiritual life. He had humility,
faith, chastity, and poverty. But the enemy, Satan, who gives not
rest, seduced him with the promise of exaltation. He acquiesced.
Satan promised this star of the Church what he had promised
Christ in the desert. In the desert Jesus conquered Satan—but that
does not mean that we shall all triumph over the same temptation.
We can also perish. The star, this person of ecclesiastical dignity
and high sanctity, enticed by Satan, fell into diabolic vice. Initially,
like Lucifer, *his chosen father,* he eschewed virtue in order to be like
God and sought to displace God. Valtorta continues, calling it
"less frightening to see a star plummet from the firmament than

to see Satan's spiral by which a once chosen creature falls and now imitates his chosen father."

This metamorphosis or internal fall of the heart cannot be externally perceived. The loss of faith by this ecclesiastical star in God's firmament, and his fall, will be well disguised. Heaven, however, will see it with horror.

This foretelling of Valtorta has a parallel in Benson's novel. A cardinal becomes a traitor and reveals that the Pope, following the destruction of Rome, has gone into hiding in Nazareth. While Benson identifies the Antichrist with a political figure, Felsenburgh, he also introduces into the plot the character of the new Judas, albeit as a minor figure. Maria Valtorta regards the "star in God's firmament" as the Antichrist in person. According to Valtorta, "Lucifer, through pride, became erased and obscure. The Antichrist, in an hour of pride, for a very short period, will become the accursed and the obscure, having been a star in my army." This is an ecclesiastic, a perverted saint, someone drawn from a religious background. These texts are most interesting—but that does not mean that what they contain will come to pass. What does come to pass—in Heaven and on earth—we shall see only when it happens. It is sufficient for us to persevere in the faith.

Valtorta's account continues:

Satan, as a reward for deserting to him, will give the Antichrist all the assistance and the infernal weapons needed to govern and dominate the world and so become lord of the world. He will lend him all his own weapons to conquer the world. Through the Antichrist, the whole world will be brought under the lordship of Satan. The Antichrist will lead all men to Satan. In return for his abjuration, which will shake the heavens with terror and cause the pillars of the Church to tremble in alarm, the Antichrist will obtain total assistance from Satan. He will receive the keys of the abyss so that he may throw it open. He will throw it wide open so that the instruments of terror fashioned by Satan throughout the centuries may be brought out and carry man to total destruction. They will call Satan king and follow the Antichrist. He is the only one who can open the portals of the abyss and allow the king of the depths to come out, just as Christ opened the doors of Heaven to dispense grace and pardon, which make men like unto God, and bring them to an eternal kingdom in which I am King of Kings.

The striking power which Satan gives to the Antichrist parallels that given by the Father to Christ (cf. Matt. 28:18). Remembering that Valtorta is taking "dictation," thus Christ, in the first person, speaks:

"As the Father has given me all power, so, too, Satan will give all power, especially the power to seduce and blind the devils and those, who, like their head, are corroded by the fire of ambition. In his overriding ambition not even the help of Satan will suffice and he will seek out help from the enemies of Christ who, armed with more deadly weapons, such as the passion for evil, will sow despair in the faithful. These will help him, for as long as God will not prevent it. God will reduce them to ashes by the brilliance of His aspect."

This is undoubtedly a tremendous text but we should recall St. Paul's Second Letter to the Thessalonians (2:12). Valtorta describes the Antichrist as a cleric who will go over to Satan and have his complete support as well as that of the enemies of Christ. More than this Valtorta does not say. She repeats the same description in other parts of her writings.

Having identified the Antichrist in the writings of Maria Valtorta we now turn to another question: will the appearance of the Antichrist coincide with the end of the world? This is an interesting question. Maria Valtorta's reply differs from that of Benson and from the more reliable tradition which places the appearance of the Antichrist at the end of the world. A close reading of Valtorta's writings reveals a rather different view of things: the Antichrist will not manifest himself at the end of the world. Rather, he will be the penultimate manifestation of evil. The defeat of the Antichrist will be followed by a period of peace in which man will return to God. In a spiritual interpretation, this period could be described as the kingdom of God on earth. It will consist not so much in a return of Christ as in a return of man to God. There will be a prolonged period of peace until the final battle in which the Antichrist appears, who will be Satan himself and will no longer appear as a man. We should remember that the word "antichrist" means one who opposes Christ. We know that he who opposes Christ is Satan. He will gather all men from the ends of the earth for the final revolt and this will truly be the supreme trial. There will be loss of faith and charity. It will be a time of great perseverance and courageous witness for Christians. Then history will end.

Valtorta's perspective has the manifestation of the Antichrist not as the final act of history but as its penultimate act. Soloviev also emphasizes this point in his *Tale.* This is an important point to emphasize, for it has influenced much of contemporary literature.

I shall omit the various passages in which Valtorta stresses that the death of the Antichrist does not coincide with the end of the world. I would mention, however, that texts written by persons still living, and who shall remain anonymous, are in circulation and promote presumed private revelations. These often repeat the intuitions of Maria Valtorta—we shall call them intuitions, as we do not wish to take any position with regard to whether or not these constitute revelations. This somewhat clandestine literature is currently in wide circulation among the faithful both in Italy and abroad. It tends to identify the Antichrist with a religious dignitary and not with a layman or politician. The Antichrist is described as a man of the Church, a false pastor. Although clothed as a lamb he is in reality a raging wolf. As Revelation puts it, he resembles the beast which is similar to a lamb but which has the voice of a dragon. He sets out to infiltrate the Church by Masonry and to exercise his task of preaching a false Christ and a false Church.

On the question of the relationship between the coming of the Antichrist and the end of the world, recent literature takes up Valtorta's theme of the manifestation of the Antichrist not coinciding with the end of the world. His appearance will signal a great crisis, especially for the Church. It will be a crisis of purification in which only the "little flock" will remain faithful. Apart from this, it will be the "crisis of the cross," so as to speak, in which there will be a new resurrection for the Church and the advent of the civilization of love. It will be period of peace and of return to God for the world—until the final trial.

It should be mentioned that contemporary literature also posits a link between the appearance of the Antichrist and the third secret of Fatima. (Although these writings are sometimes referred to as private revelations, I prefer to employ the term "literature" since in this particular field it is impossible to distinguish the wheat from the tares, at least until such time as the Magisterium of the Church does so.) The third secret of Fatima is believed to allude to a crisis of faith in the Church and to the manifestation of the Antichrist from within the Church. He intends to set up a false Christ and a false Church which will last until the crisis is overcome by the faithful flock: Mary's people. The defeat of the Antichrist will coincide with the triumph of the Immaculate Heart of Mary.

This is a complex picture. Soloviev and Benson better reflect an established tradition and are more clearly in line with the biblical texts which see the Antichrist in political terms and situate him at the end of the world. In this respect, we have seen that Soloviev reflects a certain millenarian outlook. We have also seen and underlined some important changes which have occurred in the literature during the past fifty years.

Having made these remarks, I would like to emphasize a very interesting point which has surfaced in Benson's novel, and more recently in the writings of Maria Valtorta. The manifestation of the Antichrist should happen shortly, indeed within a few years. While Soloviev merely alludes to a recognizable chronology of events, Benson sets an exact date for the manifestation of the Antichrist: 1998. This is not the year of the Antichrist's death but the year in which Felsenburgh promulgates a law obliging everyone in the world to renounce God, profess atheism, and believe in the God-Man, who is the manifestation of the Antichrist.

Maria Valtorta gives no date for the coming of the Antichrist. However, writing in 1943 she was in no doubt that the perpetrators of the rapine, violence, ferocity, and hatred unleashed by the Second World War were the precursors of the Antichrist. There were people living in 1943 who would see the advent of the Antichrist. From this we can infer that Valtorta believed that the Antichrist would be manifested at the close of this century. This same reference to the end of this century also occurs in some of the contemporary literature to which we have referred. This literature speaks of the appearance of the Antichrist before the year 2000.

Amongst these texts there is a strange convergence on the date of the Antichrist's appearance. It would seem that the manifestation is actually happening in these very years and will break out of its fetters in the immediate future.

We must not forget that we have been speaking of two novelists and of a number of private revelations, about which the Church has made no pronouncements. Hence, we are dealing with assertions which must be approached with the utmost caution.

This overview has been of interest, if for no other reason than the large following which Valtorta and such other writers as we have examined have. Faced with such a proliferation of prophetic writing about the Antichrist and the end of the world, I believe that it would be useful to present the faithful with the criteria doctrinally established by which such texts can be evaluated. These criteria are based on the Word of God and are outlined in the *Catechism of the Catholic Church*.

Personally speaking, my own outlook is very simple: it is inspired by the spirituality of the Bible which calls us to "watch" and to "pray" because the future is in God's hands. A careful reading of the signs of the times in the light of the Word of God is also necessary. Because we are so close to the year 2000, these are special times. Benson's novel can be useful in this endeavor. In all honesty, I have to say that neither the teachings of Maria Valtorta (what authority can be ascribed to her?) nor the more recent "revelations" have impressed me. In these cases we always have to ask what authority can be ascribed to them. Until such time as the Magisterium of the Church decides in these matters, accepting them would be like building on sand.

One document, however, made a great impression on me and, in a certain sense, has the seal of the Church's approval. This is the diary of Sr. Faustina Kowalska. As you know, Sr. Faustina has been beatified and the revelation and devotion given to her, that of the Divine Mercy of Christ, has been approved by the Church. Here we are not saying that the Church approves Sr. Faustina's diary. However, when someone is declared a saint because of the revelation given to her and the virtues she practiced, her writings acquire a certain authority. Let us read what Jesus says to Sr. Faustina towards the conclusion of the diary: "I love Poland in a special way and if it will obey my will, I shall lift it up in power and holiness and from Poland, there will come that radiance which will prepare the world for my final coming." This is a very moving text. Ultimately, the Church has validated these revelations. We can have moral certitude that Jesus did speak to Sr. Faustina, and we cannot but think that the radiance to prepare for the second coming spoken of in this text (written in 1937 or 1938), refers to Pope John Paul II. Of course, the revelation makes no mention of dates or names. I present this interpretation merely because I could not resist making it.

However, in this regard we have to adopt the perspective of faith. History is in the hands of God. History is always filled with God's surprises. The Christian cannot sleep or enjoy life thinking that the Lord might not be coming quickly. The Gospel warns of this.

Let us return to the authors we have cited. Rather than criticizing them, we should be grateful to them for what they have given us, and we should try to treasure what they teach so as to be able to read the signs of the times with a Christian attitude of watching, praying, and persevering in the faith and the spiritual struggle. Above all, we should evaluate them carefully and weigh them prudently on the basis of sure criteria.

The Wrath of God

Let us not forget that the theme of the Antichrist is not just a legend or a literary one. It is part of God's revelation and the Church's preaching. This I have already said when making the biblical and theological presentation in the introduction.

Robert Benson's analysis in *Lord of the World* is very helpful because it brings together certain aspects of contemporary society which are mentioned in the *Catechism of the Catholic Church* (675). Here is an outline of the society which accepts "the supreme religious deception ... of the Antichrist, a pseudo-messianism by which man glorifies himself in place of God and of his Messiah come in the flesh."

Before turning to the book we could ask: are we living in those times which Benson predicted almost a century ago? Are we living in a time when man glorifies himself to the extent of God and his Messiah, come in the flesh?

Dear friends, these are not times of faith. They are times of unbelief, apostasy, and persecution. We cannot predict the future. All that can be said is that those who walk with Christ need have no fear. Human history, even though difficult at times, is completely in His hands.

The Signs of the Times

Let us now examine some of the signs of the times in which we live.

Apart from the fact that we are close to the year 2000 and mere chronology suggests much, there is something more essential and more profound which calls the Church to reflection: we are living in times which have never been experienced before in the history of Christianity.

In his letter to Italy[18] Pope John Paul II spoke of the growth and progress of the faith that was seen up to a few centuries ago. This

---

[18] Pope John Paul II, letter to the Italian bishops (January 6, 1994).

was true not only of Italy, but also internationally. There followed a maturity in the Christian sense of humanity.

From about 1500 a change began to occur and a progressive dechristianization began. In our own times, it has spread everywhere. After two thousand years, the Pope calls on the Church to evangelize the world again. Our own times are special because they are times of difficulty and tribulation for the Church.

What are the essential characteristics of these times? It is a fact that a great part of the Christian world has divested itself of Christianity. For several centuries an apostasy has been taking place which is now very diffused. Increasing numbers of Christians abandon the faith, while others "change" the faith, transforming it into something entirely subjective. They make of it a form of religious sentimentalism or a superior form of "gnosis."

Either the faith is lost, in which case the result is atheism or materialism (perhaps a clearer and more logical position), or the faith is "changed" or emptied of its substance and only those of its aspects are retained which satisfy personal religious needs. When speaking to central European Christians—as I have experienced myself—we often encounter persons who declare themselves as neither practicing nor believing but who profess a faith which is a superior form of conscience. When we explore this superior conscience we discover that it consists of a vague faith in the supernatural. It is a type of "new age" religion in which the transcendental dimension is all but lost.

Considerable Dechristianization

The sole fact of widespread apostasy and loss of faith should be enough to cause some to wonder if the end times have not arrived.

I use the expression "end times" because in theological terms the "end times" are the last phase of salvation history. They encompass the period between the first coming of Christ—the Incarnation—to His second coming or return in glory. We are in the final stages of the end times and it is better to express this with the term "end times." We should not forget that several New Testament passages which refer to the words of Christ, and the reflections of St. Paul and other apostles, especially St. John, indicate as a concrete characteristic of the end times attenuation or loss of faith.

Let us not overlook the question that Jesus asked: "When the Son of Man comes, will He find any faith on earth?" (Luke 18:8). After two thousand years of Christianity, the faith seems to be weakening in the heart of man, if not indeed erased from it. This is what causes us to wonder if we have not arrived at the conclusive phase of history.

Acceptance of Non-Christian Thought in the Church

A further important factor gives rise to this question. It is complementary to the preceding point and parallel to it: the crisis within the Church. If we consider the words of Jesus about the end of time in the Gospel, chapter three of Revelation, and other New Testament texts about false prophets, we have to notice that in these scriptural texts a decline of faith is not the only condition associated with the end times. Falsification of the truth at the heart of the "sacred place," which is the Church, is also mentioned.

Today, abandonment of the faith is accompanied not only by widespread atheism but also by an intra-worldly view of life. At the very heart of the Church, more or less visible forms of heresy are born and spread. Paul VI noted that within the Church there is an acceptance of non-Christian philosophies. This is something more pernicious for the Church than any external attacks on the faith fueled by a noticeable return of paganism. This is an attempt by the world to insinuate itself into the very heart of the Church and to reduce the very substance of Christianity to a non-transcendent religion.

In the final analysis, this attempt, under different forms, can be reduced to a denial of the mystery of Christ and to an insistence that He is merely a man. Once the mystery of Christ has been denied, it is quite easy to deny the mystery of the Trinity, the mystery of the Eucharist, the supernatural origin of the Church, eternal life and all the fundamental mysteries of the Christian faith. The Christological mystery and with it the entire supernatural dimension of Christianity is under attack within the Church.

Are We Close to the End?

Paul VI was insistent on two fundamental aspects of the contemporary era and wondered, especially toward the close of his pontificate, if we might not be close to the end. The answer to his question we shall never know. We must always be ready, but we might have to wait a long time. Bearing in mind the phenomena of dechristianization and the assertion of non-Christian thought in the Church, he insisted that there will always be a "little flock."

Paul VI's preoccupation with the twilight of faith in our era and the resurgence of paganism—described by Benson as "humanitarianism"—was shared by many authoritative writers, both Catholic and non-Catholic. In the 1950s Romano Guardini spoke of the end times not so much in chronological terms but as a battle between two forces—faith and the world. Giuseppe Prezzolini regarded the effort to destroy the Catholic Church as one of the most significant factors of the contemporary era. Raymond Aron, the sociologist, denounced with disquiet the rapid secularization of the Catholic Church and its accommodation with the world.

While not a believer, he maintained that this phenomenon was more significant than the agitations of 1968.

More than any other, the testimony of John Paul II reflects an understanding of this new phase of history. The idea of new evangelization—a key issue of his pontificate—implies that the world has been dechristianized. We face an era in which the faith must be proclaimed again. John Paul II is alone in conducting the battle to maintain the moral order. While the validity of this enterprise has won him some support in most quarters, it also serves to illustrate clearly the forces that are contending against him. The little flock of those who believe in Christ remains. It alone, without help from other religions, is left to defend not just the principles of the faith, but the moral order itself.

We have arrived at a very important juncture in history. It is one of crisis in faith and of persecution for the Church. It is one in which the "little flock" is called to witness and struggle while facing persecution.

I think the picture has been sufficiently outlined. We are certainly not living in a phase of Catholic triumphalism. Instead, we experience that phase of Christ's life in which He was crucified. It is perhaps through crucifixion that Christianity will experience a new spring.

What reasons exist for connecting the end times with this new phase that we are experiencing and that is marked by loss of faith, opposition from the world, and persecution? Among a certain intelligentsia, there is little doubt that great intolerance exists for the Church.

The Bible tells us that the end of the world will not be brought about by the triumph of Christianity. It foresees a battle between the forces of evil and the "little flock." The *Catechism of the Catholic Church* (675) confirms this view. "Before Christ's second coming the Church must pass through a final trial that will shake the faith of many believers." We live in an era in which the faith of many vacillates or grows dim. While we can verify that we are undergoing a crisis, we cannot know if this is the final trial. The *Catechism of the Catholic Church* adds: "The persecution that accompanies her pilgrimage on earth will unveil the 'mystery of iniquity' in the form of a religious deception offering men an apparent solution to their problems at the price of apostasy from the truth" (675). The Church has always experienced persecution in the world. It seems to me, however, that this quotation touches upon something which is very characteristic of our era, namely, today the faith of believers is put to the test. If Christians are persecuted today, the greatest test they face is seduction. The new religion proposes a synthesis of all religions.

I wonder if we are living in a time not only of crisis but also of religious persecution. Persecution is a constant factor in history. Persecution today comes in the form of the religious deception which offers "men an apparent solution to their problems." Science presumes to solve man's problems, including death, but at the cost of "apostasy from the truth." Setting aside prophecies, private revelations, and the arrival of the year 2000, these are hard facts which must cause us to ask Paul VI's question: "Are we close to the end?" The only reply to this question was given by Paul VI: "We shall never know. We have to be ready, but we may have to wait for a long while."

It would be interesting to reflect on *waiting for a long while*. We could analyze the natural resources in order to determine how much longer the world can continue to exist. We also have to remember that this world has produced thousands of atomic bombs, pollution, immorality that produces and produces and produces ... I have no faith in a world of depravity, corruption, and drugs or one in which a tiny state can produce an atomic bomb. If the world does not convert to God, how much longer can it endure?

Ultimately, we are not interested in an answer saying "Yes, we are close to the end," or "No, we are not close to the end." Both would be hypothetical. Instead, we wish to initiate a true reflection on the world in which we live, especially from a religious perspective. In this we seek to understand the signs of the times in the light of Sacred Scripture, the Magisterium of the Church, and the Saints. This should help us to understand the new and difficult situation experienced by Christianity at the present time. The faith has been put to the test. Innumerable Christians have been seduced by the religious deception which is presented as the "new religion," the religion of Aquarius. They believe that Christianity has been superseded and they think that they have passed into a superior consciousness. These poor people do not know what to say or do when confronted with the question of death and evil.

Like a great prophet, it almost seems that Benson described our own existential experience in what he calls "humanitarian religion." All religions, except Catholicism, are drawn to it. Buddhism, Hinduism, even Islam, Masonry, and many esoteric sects are attracted by "humanitarian religion." All these religions form a religion of man which will result in a type of religious imposture which declares man to be the author of his own salvation. Ultimately, it will proclaim man to be God. This is the first attack on the Church, and it comes in the form of seduction. It will be followed by persecution: all the world except for a tiny minority of Catholics, following behind the Antichrist, will be concentrated on the Church's destruction. But since the powers of Hell cannot prevail, the eradication of the Catholic Church will coincide with the second coming of Christ.

Lord of the World: An Epilogue of Biblical Character

In exploring Benson's novel we shall set aside its chronology and concentrate on those themes of interest to us. The first notable point to be made about the novel is its biblical character.

We have noted that the novel ends with a settling of accounts between two armies. The first is that of the "humanitarians" following the religious deception (to use the term employed by the *Catechism of the Catholic Church*). These deify man and deem him capable of solving all problems including death, which is seen as a return to the spirit of humanity which pervades man himself. (This solution to the problem of death was foreseen by Benson. In our times, it takes the form of a belief in reincarnation which is quite widespread.) Marshalling this army is the Antichrist who, in accordance with the biblical text, is the expression of the spirit of the world and incarnates the spirit of the age. He is highly popular and has the support of the majority.

The pope heads the opposing army. He leads a "little flock" of a few thousand who have preserved the faith.

The epilogue has the clear biblical theme of the end of time. It will not signify the triumph of the Church, the faith or of the Gospel. The end of the Church will be like that of Jesus Christ. Just as Christ ended His earthly life in abandonment, persecution, arrest, betrayal, the ignominy of the passion, so too will it be for His people. Reduced to a little flock, Christians will be persecuted and crucified. Thus the Church will arrive at the end of time and relive the Lord's passion. The *Catechism of the Catholic Church* notes:

> The Church will enter the glory of the kingdom only through this final Passover, when she will follow her Lord in His death and Resurrection. The kingdom will be fulfilled, then, not by a historic triumph of the Church through a

progressive ascendancy, but only by God's victory over the final unleashing of evil, which will cause His Bride to come down from Heaven. God's triumph over the revolt of evil will take the form of the Last Judgment after the final cosmic upheaval of this passing world. (677)

Benson's book revolves around the clear biblical teaching substantially formulated in the *Catechism of the Catholic Church*. The Church will relive the Lord's passion. I believe that the final part of the book is truly inspired. The powers of the world, led by the Antichrist, descend in a squadron of aircraft on the village of Nazareth to destroy Silvester, the last pope. He has taken refuge in a hovel at Nazareth. The Pope and few thousand Catholics scattered throughout the world are the last remaining faithful. Following the destruction of Rome, the final act to be consummated by the armies of the Antichrist is the extermination of the "little flock" which survived, but which is destined for crucifixion. At the time, the real Lord of the World, Jesus Christ, will come.

To my mind, this aspect of Benson's novel helps to clarify many ideas. Given that the book was written many years before the *Catechism of the Catholic Church*, it would be irreverent to suggest that Benson (a man of deep religious culture, a Catholic priest, and a convert) might not have had some influence on the formulation of the passage that we have cited from the *Catechism of the Catholic Church*. Very few authors have understood as well as Benson the significance of the Church's exact reliving of the events of Christ's life at the end of the world. But since the gates of Hell shall not prevail, the destruction of the last "little flock" will coincide with the second coming of Christ. As the *Catechism of the Catholic Church* notes, the final coming of Christ "will take the form of the last Judgment." This is a datum of the faith. In his novel Benson has reproduced a conception of history which is heavily inspired by the faith.

Betrayal of Believers and Growth of Apostasy

Since the Church of the end times will be reduced to a "little flock" before being persecuted, of interest to us is an explanation for the tremendous crisis and the growth of apostasy. This theme certainly interests us. How can it come about that Christianity, which once formed entire civilizations, will be reduced to a "little flock"? Here we are not theorizing or talking of a literary fiction. We are treating of facts which can be universally verified. It is a fact that Christians are numerically in a minority. A progressive reduction in the number of believers can be seen everywhere—or at least in Western societies. Christianity has collapsed and must be equated with the "few."

Benson reflected on this and offers an opinion which must cause us to think: if deception and apostasy are growing it is because Christians have betrayed the faith. While the implications of this are grave, they must be faced with all their consequences. For Benson, the reduction of the Church to a "little flock" comes about through the betrayal of Christians who, having absorbed Christianity, become tired of the faith and behave as the Galatians of whom Paul says:

> Are you people in Galatia mad? Has someone put a spell on you, in spite of the plain explanation you have had of the crucifixion of Jesus Christ? Let me ask you one question: was it because you practiced the Law that you received the Spirit, or because you believed what was preached to you? Are you foolish enough to end in outward observances what you began in the Spirit? Have all the favors you received been wasted?" (Gal. 3:1-4)

In a conversation in the novel, Benson asks the question: was the fall of the Church a consequence of having lost faith or was it its cause? He replies that the fall of the Church was brought about by loss of faith. The faithful rejected the faith. They fell because of internal collapse. The religious deception is well advanced.

Benson maintains an important thesis: the Church cannot be broken by external persecution. Tertullian was correct. External persecution strengthens the Church. "The blood of martyrs is the seed of Christians." The Church falls because of internal betrayal and infidelity.

To what are these infidelities due? They are provoked by the corruption in us—the poison injected into us by the serpent. They are due to our desire to diminish God and replace Him with ourselves and our desire for this world.

Benson advances some very provocative reasons for the loss of faith. He summarizes them in a few brilliant lines—we should recall that the novel, written in 1907, is situated towards the end of the twentieth century and reviews an era which, in reality, is our own.

> The Bible was completely given up as an authority after the renewed German attacks of the twenties; and the Divinity of Our Lord, some think, had gone all but in name by the beginning of the century. The kenotic theory had provided for that.

Benson gives two verifiable reasons for the dissolution of the faith. One is a certain form of exegetical theology which, seen in itself as an application of science to the study of the Bible, reduces the Bible to a book like all others and the Word of God becomes a human word. The Holy Spirit, its real author, is displaced by the human author. Hence, through literary analysis and a series of

so-called scientific theories applied to the Bible, it is concluded that
the Bible is not divinely inspired nor the bearer of God's Word.

The internal dissolution of Christianity derives from a form
of science which is no longer conscious of its own limitations. It
is not subject to the Magisterium and regards itself as absolute. It
manipulates the Bible and annihilates its inspired character.

The other wound inflicted on the Church touches on the mystery of Christ. This is the "kenotic" theory. The word derives from
the Greek word *keno,* to empty, and this work *keno* is used by St.
Paul in his letter to the Philippians (2:7) when explaining how
Christ, in becoming man, freely emptied Himself not only of His
divine nature, but also of the glory which was His in virtue of that
nature. This theological theory, in emphasizing that God really
became man and stressing the humanity of Christ, plays down
the divinity of Christ. According to the theory, Jesus Christ is no
longer God. He is merely a great representative of God and one
of the many "saviors" of man.

Benson reacts with biting polemic against this theology which
could be called "modernist."

On the subject of the internal dissolution of the faith, he notes
that in those times before the appearance of the Antichrist—in
preparation for his arrival—a movement emerged called the movement of "Free Ecclesiastics" which was similar to many contemporary movements:

> Then there was that strange little movement among the Free
> Churchmen even earlier: when ministers who did no more
> than follow the swim—who were sensitive to draughts, so
> to speak—broke off from their old positions. It is curious
> to read in the history of the time how they were hailed as
> independent thinkers. It was just exactly what they were not.

This is admirable foresight. In 1907 Benson envisaged many of the tendencies of the age: a form of biblical criticism which erodes the authority of the Bible as a sacred book; a form of Christianity which leads to denial of the divinity of Christ; a desire for emancipation on the part of a clergy which no longer perceives its supernatural state, loses its identity, abandons celibacy, and becomes absorbed by the world. We experienced these phenomena in the 1970s when the Church lost eighty thousand of some four hundred thousand priests. They left the ministry conquered and deluded by what Benson would describe as the common cultural currents. Here Benson is truly a prophet of a great tragedy which would afflict the Church. Who among us does not know one of these priests? Without wishing to mention names, we can recall the 1970s when these priests dominated our television screens and made the front pages of the newspapers. They were hailed for their independence of mind. In truth, however, they were merely slaves to the common mentality of the times—as Benson prophetically described it.

These events illustrate the tragedy which we are living. In his novel, Benson speculated about Christianity, which had constructed a great western civilization but was now reduced to minority status. It was displaced by a form of religion which denies the supernatural, which is betrayed by Christians themselves. These have struck at the nerve center of the faith—the divinity of Christ, biblical revelation, and the authority of the Magisterium. They have destroyed the discipline of the clergy and of religious. They have dissolved the faith from within.

This crisis has reduced the Church to a "little flock." We have seen the adroit emphasis in Paul VI's observation: "There is a growing non-Christian thought in the Church."

On this point Benson unleashes a fierce criticism of intellectuals. In the face of the Church's attempt to impose discipline through the general Council, he says that there will be a great exodus of intellectuals from the Church because they will no longer recognize her faith or her discipline. The "little flock" will remain faithful. It will be a little flock comprised of little people and of the humble. The intellectuals will depart to assist the Antichrist. In this, too, Benson was a prophet.

Is everything negative then? No, dear friends. Benson, having analyzed the reasons for the collapse of the Church, concludes by saying: "I mean ... that the severing of the sheep and the goats had begun." As Jesus said: let the wheat and the tares grow together until the end of the world when the separation will take place (cf. Matt. 13:30).

The Point of the Situation

Up to now, we have explored two great prophecies in Benson's novel. It would be interesting to discover the extent to which they have been corroborated in our own times.

The first of these prophecies envisages a great simplification of the religious panorama in the course of history: on the one hand, Catholicism, reduced to a tiny flock, ready to resist and fight unto death. On the other, all religions are absorbed by the so-called humanitarianism. The end of the world will see the appearance of the Antichrist who is a product of humanitarianism. He will unleash his attempt to eradicate the Catholic Church. There is no doubt that the teaching of the Bible and of the Catholic Church envisages a dramatic end for the world. The battle of the two "cities," as St. Augustine calls them, will take place. There will be persecution and an effort to destroy the Catholic Church. The end times will not see the Church triumphant. Instead, they will bring her persecution and crucifixion. The Church will share in the lot of her founder. Then with the coming of the Redeemer, the Church will rise. Here Benson illustrates how clearly he has understood the teaching of the New Testament. Now we can inquire as to the extent to which the prospect outlined by Benson has been actualized.

At this point, it seems to me that Benson's prediction is only partially fulfilled. Humanitarianism has not absorbed all religions in the world. Among religions, Catholicism represents a strong reminder of the supernatural. It remains to be seen whether Islam, with its ardent faith in God, will be assimilated to humanitarianism. Benson believed that Islam had also developed esoteric forms and was thus infiltrated by humanitarianism. With regard to Islam there may well be surprises in the future. It maintains the strongest intuition of man's submission to God. It remains unclear how a religion such as Islam, which is strongly imbued with a sense of God's transcendence, could be absorbed by humanitarianism. This is even more true of its fundamentalist forms that are currently flourishing and are so markedly hostile to the neopaganism of Western civilization.

Islam may be an exception to Benson's prophecy which envisages the absorption of all religions into humanitarianism. We do not know what role God has given to Islam in His plan. While it is irreconcilable with Christianity because of its denial of Christ's divinity and the dogma of the Trinity, its opposition to atheistic Marxism must be acknowledged.

I am convinced that oriental religions such as Buddhism, Hinduism, and Confucianism will be absorbed by the religion of humanitarianism. Such religions fail to maintain a distinction between God and man and end in proclaiming the divinity of man and his capacity to save himself. It would not be surprising to see the religions of the East assimilated by the religion of humanism at some point in the future. The point is illustrated by the manner in which many of the orphans of Western Marxism have adopted Oriental religions. This suggests a certain common basis. It is a move from a form of materialistic atheism to a spiritualistic atheism which is conducted within the context of an immanentism which denies God and identifies man with God.

While it is certain that there will be a final battle, the question remains whether it will be conducted between Catholicism and humanitarianism. In this, what role will Islam, with its millions of followers throughout the world, play? Will it preserve its faith or will it be assimilated to humanitarianism? Rather than being an enemy of Catholicism, could the day come when Islam will be its ally in affirming the transcendence of God, His primacy, and His supremacy with regard to man? Islam is truly a mystery in God's plan.

Benson's prophecy concerning the internal dissolution of the Church indicates that he truly understood the significance of denying the Bible as an inspired book, denying its principal authorship by the Holy Spirit, denying Christ's divinity in order to assert His humanity, the mass defection from the priesthood, the birth of modernism, and the exodus of intellectuals from the Church. There is no denying that the Church has undergone a severe crisis and experienced these trials during recent decades. Paul VI warned of the rise of a certain "non-Christian outlook" within the Church.

Both of Benson's prophecies, with certain qualifications, have, in some ways, been fulfilled in our own times.

The Content of Humanitarian Religion

Here we shall attempt an analysis of that religious phenomenon which is fundamental to Benson's prophecy and to which we have frequently referred, namely, humanitarianism — in many ways a precursor of modernity.

The Wrath of God

At the beginning of this century, Benson saw the gradual emergence of a new religion which proposed man, instead of God, as the object of worship.

The humanitarian religion described by Benson is anything but a utopia. In the last century, the French philosopher Auguste Comte became known for this proclamation of a humanitarian religion which was dedicated to the worship of man. The intellectual pursuit of the 18th century has become mass religion in our own times. The course of this century has witnessed the emergence of certain dangerous forms of the humanitarian religion. Marxism worshipped society, the state symbols of the party, Lenin, Stalin, and Mao. Nazi Germany deified the state and Hitler.

Nevertheless, that type of humanitarian religion foreseen by Benson at the end of the last century, whose enemy is Catholicism and which must be overcome at all cost, is now widespread and indeed a mass phenomenon. Through one of his characters, Benson describes it: "Humanitarianism ... is becoming an actual religion itself, though anti-supernatural. It is Pantheism." Pantheism deifies all nature, god is the world, but naturally, man above all is god since he is the highest expression of nature. It is a religion devoid of the *super*natural, because since nature itself is god, there is no longer a distinction between Creator and creature. The creature is god and hence arbitrator of his own destiny and establishes the moral law for himself. Nature, and man as its highest expression, has all the divine attributes. Humanitarianism is a religion devoid of the supernatural.

It is developing a ritual under Freemasonry; it has a creed, "God is man"; and the rest. It has, therefore, a real food of a sort to offer religious cravings: it idealizes, and yet makes no demands upon the spiritual faculties. Then, they have the use of all the churches except ours, and of all the Cathedrals; and they are beginning at last to encourage sentiment. Then they may display their symbols and we may not: I think they will be established legally in another ten years.

Decline of the True Faith and the Emergence of the "Religious"

The atheist world will not lack religion. When we hear today that we are present at the rebirth of the spiritual and faced with a need for religious symbols, we must ask what religion is being born. If we mean a religion based on man's perennial need for the divine in some vague sense, then we can agree with the foregoing. However, this cannot be mistaken for a rebirth of the faith. Paradoxically, we are experiencing a decline of the true faith and a renaissance of the "religious," understood in Benson's sense of the word. This is a religion devoid of the supernatural. It consists of a complex of pantheistic beliefs which, today, are regarded as "new age" or as something with the same immanent characteristics. Man is at the epicenter of their new religiosity. It celebrates men of superior power. While having its symbols and cult, it is completely confined to the finite, to human possibility and to human thought. This religion is deeply influenced by esoteric forms of Masonry and by oriental religions.

It is a fundamental tenet of "new age" religion that we are entering a new era in which the religions of the past will be subverted and, in some way, assimilated. It is also intended to absorb Christianity, which is regarded as a barbaric religion to be overpowered. Christianity is regarded as a religion no longer fit for modern man. It must be purged of its fundamental dogmas and eventually reinterpreted. These are not merely prophecies. In many instances, they are already realities.

The Wrath of God

Unfortunately, we live among Christians who dedicate themselves to evacuating the Catholic faith of its content so as to reinvent it and make it relevant in the "new age" galaxy. Hence, when we speak of a religious renaissance today the term must be critically evaluated. Certainly, the faith today has its successes. There are conversions to the Gospel. The Church gains new members. I would not, however, speak of a rebirth of faith today. Perhaps it would be more true to say that there is a loss of the sense of the true faith. For those who try to present the faith, it is an uphill struggle.

Atheism is the religion of the future. At its root, atheism is always a negation of God and every such negation presupposes His affirmation. Rather than saying "God does not exist," a more sophisticated form of atheism will assert that "Man is god; humanity is god; god is immanent in human history and in the lives of individuals." This is a form of religion which has assimilated the characteristics of a true religion. Adore man and satisfy the religious needs present in every human heart. Do not renounce the Kingdom of God; construct it, instead, on earth. Just as the Catholic religion tries to unite all men under a supernatural principle represented in the person of the Vicar of Christ, so too, humanitarianism strives to unite all men and to conciliate all religions. It seeks to institute universal peace by recognizing the supreme unifying authority of the Antichrist—perfect image of the immanent god in the world, the man-god. God did not become man. The man-god is the savior of the world.

This gives rise to some interesting thoughts. We are not, as previously held, moving towards a period of atheism marked by the death of God and the disappearance of religion. Do you recall the Marxist prophecies? According to Feuerbach and Marx, religion is induced by man's social suffering and by his oppression and

manipulation. Man consoles himself with God. Once man has a
happier earthly life, God will suddenly disappear. Religion is no
more than the creature's attempt to console himself for a lack of
earthly solace. Marxism prophesied a future in which man will
satisfy all his human needs and enjoy paradise on earth. Such will
result in the demise of faith in God. Paradise will be achieved by
peace, progress, and labor for all. Indeed, some sociologists predicted the demise of religion in society. In my own youth, I read
books on the subject of the death of religion.

Today, however, we notice a curious rebirth of the "religious" —
not of "religion" but of the "religious." It is interesting to note that
there are more magicians than priests in Italy at the present time,
and what happens in Italy is a good reflection of what is happening
elsewhere. The figure of the priest as minister of the supernatural
is dying while the image of the magician, minister of natural or
dynamic forces, is growing.

Benson had greater foresight. At the turn of the century, he
clearly perceived that the crisis of faith will not be followed by the
growth of atheism but by the rise of a new religion which deifies
man. In some of his best writing, he gives concrete expression to
man's need to adore someone. The new religion will have its own
ministers of cult, its own rites and ceremonies, and its own books
to celebrate those rites. Churches and abbeys will be transformed
into temples of the new religion of humanitarianism and the Mass
will be displaced by the celebration of the new rites. The statue
of Christ will disappear and in its place the statue of "man" will
be raised up in the form of "Apollo," symbol of corporeal beauty
and virility. The statues of "maternity" and "fertility" will replace
those of Our Lady. Former priests will defect to the new religion.
They will preside over the ceremonies of the new religion. While
churches in which Christ is still adored and Our Lady honored

will be empty, those of the new religion will be filled to capacity. (This is a very vivid prediction especially when we see today's empty churches.)

Man will go to church to worship himself. He will incense the altar of his own "virility" and the statue of "maternity" and "continuous life." The crisis of faith is the crisis of the supernatural. Man no longer believes in something beyond his own reason. He no longer believes in a God whom he cannot measure or control and who is different from him.

The "new age" phenomenon corresponds exactly to the growth of the new humanitarian religion which denies a transcendent God and exalts man and his resources into an absolute. I have come to these conclusions following diverse encounters after which it became clear to me that these phenomena are not just unpalatable symptoms or merely liberal theories current in contemporary culture. They are already part of the thought process of the masses. They are mass phenomena. I have encountered Catholics who will calmly announce that they have arrived at a "superior form of religion" which corresponds to humanitarianism. They no longer have faith in God, in Jesus Christ, the Son of God, and in grace. Instead of praying, they search for unknown forces and the vital powers of the occult. Transcendental meditation substitutes for prayer. Through introspection, which it facilitates, they search for the traces of God in themselves.

With all of this it is perhaps useful to recall what Benson had to say of "prayer" in the age of humanitarianism. It is a meditation which, in the final analysis, is an immersion into self, a staying in self or a deification of self. Prayer of this kind lacks all transcendence. Today, it is not necessary to go far to find Christians who have become "humanitarians." Perhaps some of our friends are even among them.

Who Is the Antichrist?

Defining the Antichrist's identity is a central preoccupation of Benson's novel. The topic gives rise to much discussion. Many questions could be asked about the Antichrist's identity. Is the Antichrist a concrete person or does he merely represent an ideology, the spirit of the age, or a mass reality? Is the Antichrist to be defined in two alternative ways: a single person or a collective phenomenon? Benson offers a very probable and intelligent solution for this problem. The Antichrist is both. The person of the Antichrist is manifest at the center of the great schism of man from God. He is at the heart of man's self-deification. He is the one whom Paul calls "the man of iniquity." He is the supreme manifestation of humanitarian religion. It is impossible to separate the Antichrist from the specific context of apostasy, loss of faith, and rebellion against God. A central theme of the novel is the view that the Antichrist is like a flower that needs a specific environment to flourish and, outside it, fails. This point is of interest to our present purpose. For man it is a marvelously scented flower. It is the supreme self-revelation of God. For Christians, however, it is *the man of iniquity*. I am convinced that Christians should free themselves from the idea that the Antichrist can come from anywhere, Heaven or Hell, and that he will manifest himself as an evil person who will impose his dominion by force. Dear friends, the contrary is the case. The Antichrist will appear in a very specific context—that of the triumph of the spirit of the world in the form of the religion of man. From a human point of view, he will be a fascinating person. From a natural perspective he will be the best human being produced by nature. He will be proclaimed as Lord and God by all the churches of the world which he will have reordered for the adoration of man. Everything will be done through conviction and not through force.

With the eyes of faith, we can see him as the incarnation of the Devil and the supreme manifestation of evil. From a worldly perspective, however, he will be regarded as one of the greatest men ever to have been born. He will possess an incredible power to seduce man. He will possess in himself a fascination for everything beautiful that nature has ever produced. For this reason, perhaps, Christians will find it difficult to see him for what he is.

A Portrait of the Antichrist

In a biographical sketch of Julian Felsenburgh, Benson delineates the personality of the Antichrist. He is someone who presents himself to the world with all the characteristics and prerogatives of divinity:

> Felsenburgh was the creator, for it was reserved for him to bring into being the perfect life of union to which all the world had hitherto groaned in vain; it was in His own image and likeness that He had made man. Yet He was the Redeemer too, for that likeness had in one sense always underlain the tumult of mistake and conflict. He had brought man out of darkness and the shadow of death, guiding their feet into the way of peace.

For these and other reasons Felsenburgh was "savior—the Son of Man, for He alone was perfectly human."

> He was the absolute, for He was the content of ideals; the Eternal, for He had lain always in nature's potentiality and secured by His being the continuity of that order; the Infinite, for all finite things fell short of Him who was more than aware of their sum. He was Alpha, then, and Omega, the beginning and the end, the first and the last. He was Dominus et Deus noster.

We should note at this point, that the title *dominus et deus noster*—our lord and god—was first used by the Emperor Domitian who is alluded to in Revelation as the great persecutor of Christians. The biography of Felsenburgh ends with a peroration about him:

> "Behold I am with you always [says Felsenburgh the Antichrist] even now in the consummation of the world; and the comforter is come unto you. I am the Door—the Way, the Truth and the Life—the Bread of Life and the Water of Life. My name is Wonderful, the Prince of Peace, the Father Everlasting. It is I who am the Desire of All Nations, the Fairest amongst the children of men—and of my kingdom there shall be no end."

This extraordinary and seductive personality possessed the highest merits, as far as the human race was concerned. From the obscure politician that he was—we know that he was an American, but we shall not hold that against him—Felsenburgh presented himself as the master of fifteen languages. He knows the depths of the human heart. For the first time in history, mankind is assured of history. His will be a universal reign of justice, peace, and progress. Thanks to the elimination of discord among peoples and nations, the commitment of mankind to progress, and his self-revelation, the Antichrist is proclaimed as "Lord and God" in thousands of churches throughout the world.

Benson presents a positive image of the Antichrist. It is a portrait of a politician of high human qualities. He is calm, serene, educated, a pacifist and a universalist. He can bring people into the way of justice, prosperity, and peace. There will be no more misery or violence at the time of his appearance. Instead, there will be perfect concord and fulfillment of the materialist ideal as well as that of Masonry and communism.

Catholicism alone will resist him. How then do we destroy this superstition which alone obstructs the world's self-revelation? How do we destroy this superstition that divides mankind and prevents man from being truly brotherly and free?

The true Antichrist is revealed in the replies to these questions. Here is perceived his profound being as the *man of iniquity*. He will not tolerate the idea of men who adore any god other than himself. His intolerance obliges him to make an exception to his pacifism and his philosophy of non-violence. He is the greatest pacifist in the history of the human race, but because peace and justice really reign on earth he will make an exception to kill and destroy the great superstition of Catholicism, once and for all time. Reacting against a group of English Catholics who attack the cult of "humanity" — observed in former Catholic churches — he exposes the leaders of the plot to massacre. He orders his planes, drawn from the nations of the world, to concentrate on Rome and completely destroy it. Rome will be the only city to remain faithful to the Pope, who governs it according to Catholic principles. The city will be a refuge for those Catholics who refuse to accept the "law of profession," as the Antichrist calls it, which obliges the citizens of the world to renounce the Christian God and profess belief in man's divinity. The same law provides for a profession of belief in the divinity of the Antichrist's representative, Julian Felsenburgh. Pope, cardinals, and faithful must all be exterminated during the air raid.

But a cardinal was absent from Rome and escaped annihilation. Elected Pope, he guides the last vestiges of Catholicism, with the aid of another cardinal, from the village of Nazareth. Then the Antichrist makes another exception to his pacifism to consummate the last act of violence and kill the reigning pontiff — it will be the last act of violence in history, for after it comes peace

and progress, at which point, dear friends, the end of the world
will come.

Benson's analysis seems convincing to me. We tend to think
of the Antichrist in theological terms and with the eyes of faith.
Paul refers to him as the man of iniquity who displaces God and
desires to be worshipped. John describes him as the beast similar
to the panther and the beast that resembles a lamb but has the
voice of a dragon. We know that the Antichrist is the representative of the infernal dragon, and we expect him to manifest himself
with the terrible marks and characteristics of the Devil. Benson,
however, imagines the Antichrist disguised as the perfect man,
possessed of all the positive qualities which bring worldly success.
This renders his enormous power of seduction—which is ascribed
to the Antichrist by Scripture—very plausible. The identification
of the Antichrist with a politician is very interesting. We should
note, however, that in Benson's character, the political and the
religious are one and united. The Antichrist is a politician and
a man of universal peace. He demands absolute worship of himself—indeed, he demands a true and proper religious adoration.
Benson believes that it is necessary to unite these two interpretations of the Antichrist (concrete person and ideology). In order
to manifest himself, the Antichrist needs the specific context of
an atheistic, materialistic society that has lost faith in God and is
already prepared to fall down and worship man.

Man must be adored, and, at the propitious moment, the Antichrist will appear. He will preach the Gospel of the World with
an extraordinary facility for seduction. He will offer the same
promises Satan did when he tempted Christ. The Antichrist will
accept Satan's proposal to become king of the world and to build
the Kingdom of God on earth. For those who worship the true
God, there will no longer be any escape.

The Wrath of God

Lord of the World: Social Criticism or Prophecy?

At this point in our presentation of Benson's book, we can ask if the book is not to be "deconstructed." Is this simply a product of the imagination? Is it a social critique or is it indeed a work of prophecy, not so much in the sense that it makes particular revelations, but in the sense that it intuits the direction taken by society and, from present trends, is able to foresee the future?

I am certain that Benson was a forceful critic of his contemporary society and of its ideologies. However, he is also a great prophet of the twentieth century. He gathers together those seeds which would germinate and grow in our own times—especially those of the Second World War. These seeds have now grown into trees and are clear for all to see.

His primary merit was to have understood, in 1907, that for the first time in history, atheism was not the religion of the few. Atheism had always been the preserve of a small intellectual elite. But Benson grasped that it had become a mass phenomenon in the twentieth century—as subsequently became clear with the emergence of communism and Nazism.

Benson also realized something else about atheism: rather than remaining at the simple level of negation of God, atheism assumed the various attributes of religion and specifically those of the religion of man. Benson's prophecy of 1907 has come true today. The great religions of the world, especially oriental religions, are entering a new phase. Even Buddhism and Hinduism do not hesitate before the prospect of deifying man, affirming his divinity and closing the circle of total immanentism. All that exists is *this* universe and *this* man. The human soul is God. Man must be worshipped. Perhaps—and we have already underlined it—the limit of Benson's prophecy which postulates the coming together of all religions in humanitarian religion is to be found in his not having foreseen the probable resistance of Islam. Islam has a clear idea of the transcendent and of the distinction between creature and Creator. The very word "Islam" means submission. It presupposes an unbreachable distinction between creature and Creator, which is absent in oriental religions.

The new age phenomenon of the age of Aquarius is regarded as a new phase in history. It is an ensemble—a galaxy—of religious experiences held together by a common denial or negation of the supernatural. New Age and its dependent religious forms do not exclude those whom we call "direct heirs" of the extra worldly experience. The "extra worldly experience" of New Age, however, is very much situated in this world. It is encapsulated by the circle of finitude and nature. Ultimately it is a form of pantheism.

Benson clearly understood this and all its consequences. Atheism would assume the form and trappings of a pantheism which deifies man. Man will no longer need God, for he will save himself and ordain the moral law for himself.

The value of this novel is not that Benson set a date for the end of the world. (This must, however, be close as Benson believes it will take place towards the end of this century— something which is also held by some contemporary private revelations.) Chronological order is not of significance in Benson's novel—it is a secondary consideration. The power of the novel lies in its capacity to predict the future. Hence, we can speak of its prophetic power. It consists in having foreseen the form which the contemporary attack on the Church would take. The great battle that Christ and the Church would have to fight at the end of time would be that against the Antichrist who had vested himself in the clothes of humanitarianism.

Indeed, the attentive reader of Benson's novel will note that he anticipated many of the characteristics which mark our own society. He introduces us to a world in which man has reached the limits of material and intellectual progress. It is a world in which everything is scientifically programmed to the single great project of the triumph of humanitarianism over every other religious or social form.

Julian Felsenburgh, the Antichrist who represents and incarnates the spirit of the world, eliminates war, institutes universal peace, abolishes poverty, pollution, noise, and eventually suffering by the introduction of his euthanasia legislation. Thus he pretends to rid man of the evils that oppress him by his own power. In this Benson anticipates the great seduction of the modern world which can do nothing without God, Christ, the Church, and grace.

At the same time, he also warns of a great danger for the Church which has to do with the "great seduction"—the "great prostitute" the book of Revelation calls it—that is, humanitarian religion. Only the Church, reduced to a tiny flock, will resist. The Church will be tempted to follow the path of humanitarianism which would reduce Christianity to a form of humanism in which Christ is regarded merely as a man—although the greatest man ever born. In contemporary parlance, this form of the greatest seduction is called "secularization," or the abandonment of the supernatural dimension of the world in thought, act, and being.

At the same time, Benson foresaw that the tiny flock—of Paul VI—would resist the reduction of Christianity to humanitarian religion and that it would be branded a public enemy of the people and of progress. It would be accused of being out of step with the times and of belonging to the Middle Ages. Thus, Benson has prophesied both the seduction and the persecution of those who would uphold the supernatural dimension of Christianity.

If we think of other forms of what Paul VI described as the smoke of Satan that had entered the Catholic Church, we discover attempts to empty Christianity of its supernatural dimension and to reduce it to a humanitarian religion. In all this, little importance is attributed to sin, grace, and the transcendent. Insistence is placed on the corporeal works of mercy alone. The Sacraments are abandoned. The supernatural is relegated to the margins. The Church is considered to be democratic, and the Magisterium is contested.

Apocalyptic Expectation or Christ's Second Coming

This is surely the most interesting aspect of Benson's novel—and I am very much aware that many like to delude themselves with apocalyptic expectations. Many groups refer to this or that so-called private revelation predicting world catastrophe, the corruption of the Church, the appearance of the Antichrist from within the Church, persecution, and finally the coming of Christ in glory to solve all problems.

Such themes in Benson's novel are peripheral to its central concern, which is the attack being mounted on the Church by the forces of evil. But why should we exclude the possibility that the end of the second millennium will coincide with the end of the world and the second coming of Christ? As I have said before, it is absolutely impossible to know the precise hour. Paul VI asked "Have we come to the end?" and to this question he gave an evangelical answer: "We shall never know." The Christian has no confidence in specific dates for the end of the world. Christ Himself has set the seal of secrecy on His second coming: "You too must stand ready, because the Son of Man is coming at an hour you do not expect" (Luke 12:40). The Christian should, therefore, set aside all fear and anxiety but remain vigilant and ready.

John Paul II's pastoral activity has set a course for the Church's journey to the third millennium. When speaking of the year 2000, he does not refer to the end of the millennium but to the second birthday of Christ. The advent of the third millennium, stripped of all apocalypticism, should be experienced as a great celebration in which the Church prepares for the end of the world while celebrating the two thousandth "birthday" of Christ.

In his encyclical *Tertio millennio adveniente* (The Coming of the Third Millennium), the Pope sets the tone for this celebration of our journey and of our waiting. It should be imbued with conversion, penance, renewal, and a rediscovery of the very foundation of Christianity—which is the person of Jesus Christ. Our waiting should not be characterized by fear for our immediate future—as some of those linked to certain prayer groups which promote private revelations are. These are preoccupied by concerns such as: "Shall I be among those saved from the destruction and from the punishment of the world?" They are obsessed by "the great tribulation," chastisement, and with some tremendous event which will befall the natural world and society. There is no shortage of prophets of doom, nor of those who listen to them in fear and trepidation as the close of the millennium approaches. These people look to the future with fear and resignation and are convinced that the great chastisement is inevitable and at hand.

This attitude is not in harmony with the Church, which under the Pope's leadership, is preparing to celebrate the feast of her Spouse with a journey of penance, renewal, expiation, and reflection on the past and on the sins that churchmen have committed so as to avoid them in the future. This spirit is far removed from those who await the catastrophes which are characteristically predicted by some groups and sects. The objection is sometimes made that we must take into account those private revelations which concur in situating the great tribulation, the great purification, and the appearance of the man of iniquity at the end of this millennium. I would like to respond to this objection by insisting that we must enter into the spirit set by the Church in *Tertio millennio adveniente*, in which John Paul II has shown great pastoral tact and eschewed all polemic against those who await catastrophe at the close of the second millennium. Indeed, John XXIII, at the opening of the Council, publicly castigated the "prophets of doom." John Paul II, speaking of the Church's immediate future, simply refers to the Church's journey of joy ("jubilee" means joy), penance, and renewal. We should be grateful that the Church has placed us on the right road. If, in spite of this, someone wishes to frighten himself with scenes of catastrophe, then so be it. The true struggle for the Church is that of Benson's novel—the attack made by the forces of evil. Our attention should not be deflected from this question. The enemy of the Church is secularization, atheism, materialism, and the hedonism of a century which has sought to eradicate God from human existence. Religion is placed at the service of man to deify him and eliminate the supernatural. Anyone superior to man or who created and saved him, gave him the moral law and the faith, is denied and reduced to a human phenomenon. Christianity will either be assimilated to the religion of the world or it must be persecuted—this is Benson's central message.

Thus far, we have emphasized two of Benson's main themes, one directed toward the Church and the faithful, the other toward the world. The Church will end its history by reliving the Passion of Christ. The Church will be abandoned, betrayed, persecuted, flogged, and put to death. But since Christ has promised that the gates of Hell shall not prevail (Matt. 16:18), the world's attempt to eradicate the Church will coincide with the final coming of Christ. The ultimate desire of the world is to substitute for God. In this Benson merely repeats the Gospel. Even after the redemption, this world—although God never ceases to love it—still inclines toward the Evil One. I should now like to develop a third theme, taken from Benson's novel, which has much religious significance. It postulates the idea that if it is true that the end of the world will see the great persecution of the Catholic Church which will be marked by seduction, a tiny flock surrounding the Pope will remain faithful. Satan's tactics operate in two ways: persecution, rage, hatred, and cruelty will be directed against the more resistant Christians while seduction will be deployed against weaker Christians.

The Seduction of the "End Times"

Benson was highly interested in this third theme. His novel describes the "seduction of the times" with profound intuition. Seduction consists of humanitarian religion which will be presented as a true and proper religious experience. Man will adore man. He will pursue the illusion of being able to create an earthly kingdom of God which will be the kingdom of Man. Such a kingdom will be based on a society of peace and progress from which all sickness, old age, death, poverty, violence, and disturbances will be banished, thanks to man's intelligence and the discoveries of technology. Man will delude himself into thinking that he no longer needs God and that he can solve the problem of happiness here on earth.

On this point Benson was evidently a great theologian. The *Catechism of the Catholic Church* takes up the same line of thought as Benson on this point. While Benson's insight is already present in the Bible, I would suggest that the *Catechism of the Catholic Church* places it under the spotlight.

In the Bible, apart from the theme of the persecution of the Church at the end of time (Jesus Himself says "They persecuted me, they will persecute you too" in John 15:20), that of the great deception is also present. The Gospels, referring to the end of time, speak of "false Christs and false prophets" (Matt. 24:24). The book of Revelation (3:11 ff) describes the seduction of those dwelling on earth.

Article 675 of the *Catechism of the Catholic Church* further explicates the content of that seduction. Under the guidance of the Holy Spirit, it explains the biblical texts and teaches the theological truths of the great "religious deception" of the end times. It will include the teachings of the false prophets and the deception of the two beasts: one similar to a panther, the other resembling a lamb but with the voice of a dragon. This deception is characterized by man's pretensions to resolve all problems by his own powers and by his apostasy from God and from the truth.

There is no doubt that this teaching of the *Catechism of the Catholic Church*, nourished as it is by the Bible, is a part of the content of the faith. Again, I would like to mention Benson's contribution to the formulation of the Catholic Church's faith. His *Lord of the World* well illustrates the whim of man's autonomy, which will stamp the end times with all its seductive powers.

At the end of the world the "mystery of iniquity" will appear not only in the form of persecution but also in the form of seduction. It will offer man an opportunity to solve all his problems at the cost of apostasy from the truth. This is a fundamental theme in Benson's novel and it corresponds most closely with the teaching of the *Catechism of the Catholic Church*. It may well prefigure what is actually happening today.

In summary, these are the three great themes of Benson's book:

- The Church will live the end times as Christ lived His own life; however, there is no allusion to His arriving at the end of His triumphant journey;
- Man has never ceased in his desire to be god of this world and to substitute for God;
- Man will attempt to build a society in which he will solve all problems and in which he will no longer need God.

The Wrath of God

Society in the Time of the Antichrist

When we speak of the times of the Antichrist, naturally we tend to think of them as dark, and our particular psychology conditions us to regard them with horror. From the perspective of the faith, they will be especially gloomy, for they will be times of persecution, great rebellion, and pride. The world will be filled with former Catholics and with former Christians. From a materialist perspective, however, they will be splendid times.

As we have seen, the Antichrist will be a marvelous, young, seductive person. In common with Christ, he will be thirty years old. He will be calm, highly intelligent, and in perfect control of himself. From the perspective of natural virtue, he will be the perfect flower of humanity. It will seem as though he had been untouched by original sin—apart from his will which harbors a desire to be worshipped instead of God. Benson's Antichrist, Julian Felsenburgh, has every virtue—except humility. Benson teaches that spiritual pride, even when combined with every other virtue, is sufficient to turn man into the Antichrist.

Because he will be the most perfect man and, in a worldly sense, the most saintly man ever to have been born, it will be difficult for us to intuit that Felsenburgh is the Antichrist. Naturally he will play the part of the humble man and attribute divinity to man so as to make himself an object of worship.

Nobody can perceive the spiritual pride which drives Felsenburgh to oppose Christ and God. The splendor of his human virtues bewitches even Christians. The world will fall prostrate before him. He will be admired by the multitudes. He will be called the new Christ on earth. He will create an ideal society on earth.

According to Benson, the Antichrist will institute universal peace. He will unite the West. His great diplomatic skills will be deployed to avert war with the East. He will succeed in conciliating mankind by demonstrating the utility of peace. Rather than being a Hitler or a Stalin, the Antichrist will be a great pacifist.

Some statements by the Antichrist are striking in that they echo Christ, but in reality these statements are empty of their original sense. Christ said: "I have come not to bring peace to the earth, but the sword." The Antichrist says: "I bring peace, not the sword." In contrast with Christ, the Antichrist brings the peace of this world to this world. Christ did not succeed in bringing peace to the world. Christ placed men against men. Religion has caused wars. Religion creates opposition. Religion divides. Where Christ failed, the Masonic and pacifist Julian Felsenburgh, the Antichrist, will institute that universal brotherhood which Christ and Christianity never achieved.

Christ tried to eliminate poverty. Felsenburgh declares that "we have to say that he did not succeed.... After two thousand years of Christianity the poor are still with us. Indeed the founder of Christianity said that you would always have the poor." The Antichrist will succeed in eliminating the poor and he will render null the prophecy of Christ in Matthew 26:11. Poverty will be eradicated from the face of the earth and all men will enjoy prosperity in virtue of the "poverty laws" instituted by a grand alliance of communism and Masonry in the name of progress and class collaboration. These will be times of great peace and justice at the cost of apostasy from the truth. They will be accomplished by the proud presumption that man does not need God.

Thus, the Antichrist exalts his victory and the success of humanitarian religion:

> "Not peace but the sword," said CHRIST; and bitterly true
> have those words proved to be. "Not a sword but peace" is
> the retort, articulate at last from those who have renounced

CHRIST's claims or have never accepted them. The principle of love and union learned however falteringly in the West during the last century, has been taken up in the East as well. There shall be no more appeal to arms, but to justice; no longer a crying after a God Who hides Himself, but to Man who learned his own Divinity. The Supernatural is dead; rather, we know now that it never yet has been alive. What remains is to work out this new lesson, to bring every action, word and thought to the bar of Love and Justice: and this will be, no doubt, the task of years."

The world will have but one party: the party of peace and progress. Man will no longer fear the future. He will no longer fear those things which paralyzed society for centuries. "Man," concludes the Antichrist, "has groaned long enough in the travails of birth; his blood has been poured out like water through his own foolishness; but at length he understands himself and is at peace."

What are the reactions to Felsenburgh? "I saw the Son of Man, the Savior of the World ... I can trust Him for all the rest." This is exactly what article 675 of the *Catechism of the Catholic Church* contains: "The supreme religious deception is that of the Antichrist, a pseudo-messianism by which man glorifies himself in place of God and of his Messiah come in the flesh."

Now let us turn to Benson's description of Felsenburgh's impact on the world and of his success when he presents his program to the English Parliament and to the world. The newspapers of the time reported:

It seems from his words that Mr. Felsenburgh is probably the greatest orator that the world has ever known—we use these words deliberately. All languages seem the same to him; he delivered his speeches during the eight months through which the Eastern convention lasted, in no less than fifteen tongues.... He showed also ... the most astonishing knowledge, not only of human nature, but of every trait under which that divine thing manifests itself. He appeared acquainted with the history, the prejudices, the fears, the hopes, the expectations of all the innumerable sects and casts of the East to whom it was his business to speak.

This extraordinary man had always behaved with the utmost discretion in his home country, America, and was above reproof.

He has been guilty of none of those crimes—there is not one that convicts him of sin—those crimes of the Yellow Press, of corruption, of commercial or political bullying which have so stained the past of all those old politicians who made the sister continent what she has become.... Mr. Felsenburgh has not even formed a party. He, and not his underlings, has conquered. Those who were present in Paul's House on this occasion will understand us when we say that the effect of those words was indescribable.... Of his actual words we have nothing to say. So far as we are aware no reporter made notes at the moment, but the speech, delivered in Esperanto, was a very simple one, and very short. It consisted of a brief announcement of the great fact of Universal Brotherhood, a congratulation to all who were yet alive to witness this consummation of history; and, at the end, an ascription of praise to that Spirit of the World whose incarnation was now accomplished.

So much we can say; but we can say nothing as to the impression of the personality who stood there. In appearance the man seemed to be about thirty-three years of age, clean-shaven, upright, with white hair and dark eyes and brows; he stood motionless with his hands on the rail, he made but one gesture that drew a kind of sob from the crowd, he spoke these words slowly, distinctly and in a clear voice; then he stood waiting. There was no response but a sigh which sounded in the ears of at least one who heard it as if the whole world drew its breath for the first time; and then that strange heart-shaking silence fell again. Many were weeping silently, the lips of thousands moved without a sound, and all faces were turned to that simple figure, as if the hope of every soul were centered there. So, if we might believe it, the eyes of many, centuries ago, were turned on one known to history as Jesus of Nazareth.

It would undoubtedly be interesting to read Benson's description of a society liberated from God and of the social forms it would eventually assume. As we have said, the society which has recognized man as true god has realized peace and justice on earth. Progress, science and technology make earthly existence extremely comfortable. Traffic runs well. London can be crossed in twenty minutes. Noise has been eliminated. Housing, above and below ground level, is excellent. Everything, even food, is artificial. It is the perfect world. It is a world from which every possible inconvenience has been banished.

The Process Leading to the Collapse of Christianity

It is clear from this description of the perfect society that Benson is indulging in a parody of belief in progress. His message, however, is worth noting. Benson highlights and denounces a particular historical position according to which Christianity has failed in its objectives. While the founder of Christianity preached non-violence, in the course of its history Christianity has frequently witnessed or instigated violence and war. The followers of Christ, who promised peace, promote war and violence. This is the fundamental tenet of a particular outlook on the Church which, even today, is quite commonly accepted. Similar objections are made to Christianity when justice is considered. Christianity is accused of failure to institute justice.

Benson clearly perceived the rise of this outlook, and its analysis of Christianity's history. Exponents of this position clamor for the Catholic Church to be called to a kind of Nuremberg trial.[19] They regard the Catholic Church as the source of all the woes and horrors of the past two millennia. They hold the Church responsible for wars and offer the Crusades as proof of their claims. Pointing to the Inquisition, they accuse the Catholic Church of intolerance. Moreover, citing the death penalty and the persecution of heretics, they impute to the Catholic Church a lack of respect for human life, and because of its condemnation of class struggle, they blame it for the continuing presence of poverty in the world.

Benson fully realized the existence of this outlook which is certainly not occult. Its objective is to bring Catholicism to account and condemn it without appeal. Such is part of the effort to eradicate Christianity, directed against the most dangerous and best organized form of Christianity which is, of course, the Catholic Church. After two millennia, the imputation of the great pagan historian, Tacitus, is once again revived: the Christians are the enemies of the human race (*Annals*, XV, 44). The heart of the modern world, according to Benson, is imbued with the same belief.

---

[19] The trials at Nuremberg, and subsequent executions and prison sentences, were the international community's response to German war crimes committed during World War II. —Ed.

The Wrath of God

Contradictions in the Perfect Society

Let us return to the theme of the "supreme deception" and to that of the perfect society which has abolished the supernatural, deified man and which proudly asserts having resolved all of man's problems. By illustrating the contradictions inherent in the perfect society, Benson mounts a devastating critique of the Marxist-Masonic illusion of building the kingdom of God on earth.

The utopia of humanitarianism fails to eradicate ennui or boredom and death. The perfect society, that new Eden constructed by the Masons and the former communists, bores man. Man becomes bored in a society of peace, justice, and progress. He becomes uncomfortable in a society without noise, in which traffic is perfectly regulated and in which food need no longer be cooked. In this context, man becomes thoroughly bored. *Taedium vitae* overcomes him. Deified man becomes bored, yes: he experiences tedium. Benson holds that in the perfect society of the worldly kingdom of man, a special completely secular sacrament has to be instituted. In some respects, it parodies the Sacrament of Extreme Unction, or Anointing of the Sick, by which the Christian is strengthened in faith, sustained in Grace, and prepared to receive the palm of victory in the heavenly kingdom of God.

Humanitarian religion will institute its own cult, its own ministers, and its own temples which will be filled by its own faithful. It will set up statues of "humanity," "fertility," "maternity," and "virility"—just as the Greeks and Romans raised up the statues of Venus and Apollo which we see in museums today. In pagan times, such statutes expressed man's deification. Our Lady's statue will be replaced by that of the "goddess of the twelve stars." In man's apparently perfect society, what solutions are available for the problems of *taedium vitae* (boredom with life) and *horror mortis* (fear of death)? Up to the present time, psychology, which has delved the depths of the human consciousness, has not succeeded in resolving these problems.

In a society dominated by the great religious deception, a sacrament of euthanasia will be instituted to solve the problem of boredom and death. Those who so desire will be able to ask for "sweet death" and expire without pain. Special clinics, bound to absolute secrecy, will be set up. In complete anonymity, unknown even to their families, people will be able to request death. Before asking for this "sacrament" they will have to reflect for a week on whether to live or die, after which they will be able to administer to themselves, or receive from nurses who are called "sisters," the sweet sacrament of suicide.

The Church requires faith and right intention to receive the sacraments. Weariness of life will be sufficient grounds to receive the "sacrament" of euthanasia. All who are bored with life, especially the old who are close to death, will be able to request the "sacrament" of euthanasia so as to die gently. Such is euthanasia in the perfect society of the Antichrist: painless suicide, perfectly organized and protected by law. This is the response of the perfect society to the two terrible problems man has failed to resolve, boredom with a meaningless and worthless existence and the horror of death. Both are inevitable when God has been obscured.

This solution, however, is so inhuman and so alien to man that Benson amuses himself by recounting the story of the mother of the character Oliver, the Antichrist's first English disciple. At the end of her life, rather than requesting the "sacrament" of euthanasia, she secretly sends for a priest so as to receive the Sacrament of Extreme Unction. Benson's critique of this utopian society is really pungent. This society succeeds in establishing a worldly "kingdom of God." It proudly institutes peace, justice, and progress, but it fails to resolve man's fundamental questions, especially those of his infinite solitude and his fear of death. In response, the perfect society can only institute the strange "sacrament" of euthanasia.

In the course of history, it is precisely on the rocks of boredom and death that all attempts to create a godless society have foundered. When life becomes senseless, when there is an absence of transcendent ideals, when the horizon of life is closed in on itself: then man becomes bored. The prospect of death continually faces him and gnaws at him. He tries to forget the prospect of death and banish it to his unconsciousness a thousand times every day. It is like a rubber ball that will not stay below water—it keeps returning to the surface.

The Irreducible Ferocity of the Human Heart

Benson's critique is at its most incisive when demonstrating that no humanitarian can ever change man's heart. All the external splendor of this well-organized functional and progressive society is nothing but a fig leaf covering the ferocity present in man's heart. It is illusory to think that man can be changed from the outside by political or social programming. Man's heart is deeply and radically sick. Man is egotistical, violent, and belligerent.

Benson's novel recounts some terrible scenes of intolerance and violence against Catholics who are torn to pieces by the baying mob. The experts and the psychologists of the time of the Antichrist will justify these cruel outbursts by claiming that the masses need time to free themselves from the restraints of the past before they can live in peace and justice. This can take years, decades, even centuries. Worse is to come. The Antichrist, the supreme manifestation of the spirit of the world, the perfect man, will opt for violence and intolerance. He will take the decision to destroy Rome, that last city left to the Pope. He will raze it to the ground in an attempt to eradicate forever the plague of Catholicism. A miracle of Providence will spare the "little flock" of the faithful, including two cardinals. One of these will become pope and will retire to Nazareth. The Antichrist will gather his forces and his fighter planes to destroy Catholicism once and for all. This is the objective of the man of peace, progress, and tolerance. Such is the objective of the splendor of self-conscious reason. The perfect human being has recourse to the most terrible violence.

Benson's strongest criticism maintains that man alone will never succeed in changing man's belligerent heart.

Overestimation of World Messianism

The great merit and prophetic value of Benson's novel, as we have seen, consists in having announced the appearance of the Antichrist. As the *Catechism of the Catholic Church* holds, this will happen with the "great religious deception" in which man, apostatizing from the truth, will try to resolve his own problems by himself. Benson also foresaw that many Christians would be seduced by this deception. Indeed, it will fill them with rancor for Christianity, because in its history it has not solved the problems of peace, justice, and progress.

While Benson was clairvoyant in this, he was not a prophet in everything. Indeed, he overestimates the power of earthly messianism. It is true that Marxism has attempted to construct a worldly paradise in this century. We have seen attempts, inspired by the spirit of the world if not indeed by Masonry—to build societies devoid of any religious or moral influence. Presently, we find ourselves in what is called "the new world order" which seeks to build a global market whose authority is merely economic. Its politics eschews religion and the moral order. The tension between the Catholic Church and the world is an index of this new outlook whose "new world order" is freed from the constraints of religion, morality, and reason.

The Wrath of God

We have seen the facility with which religions, with the exception of Catholicism, are drawn into this new order. We are in a phase when a new world order is emerging which must be carefully examined. Dear friends, we have to speak in clear terms. What are the powers of Masonry, the market, and politics—which are substantially anti-Catholic—building? I think that Benson may have overestimated these powers. Are they promoting peace? To my mind, the new world order has given rise to numerous civil wars.

We also have to remember that Benson was writing at a time when nuclear energy had not yet been discovered. His novel was unable to take account of its potential for destruction. Today, however, we can take account of this factor which convinces us all the more that man, on his own, has created neither peace nor justice. Benson's novel explores the thesis that humanitarian religion (i.e., international Masonry) can bring about peace, justice, and progress. He describes a world of universal fraternity dominated by the hegemony of the few. Here, justice and peace are not promoted because the progress of the few is always based on the manipulation of the masses. Its horizon is not bounded by peace or justice. The possibility of nuclear or ecological disaster escalates. Previously, the Marxists and the Masons strove to bring about a new world order. Today they still strive for the same end. Market forces and armaments dominate this new order which exploits the greater part of the world.

The fundamental problems highlighted by Benson remain unanswered. In a godless society what is the meaning of life or death? On this point Benson's critique of the society of the future is somewhat superficial. He accepted as a possibility that atheistic Marxism and Masonry, acting separately and together, could realize peace and justice. In fact they have achieved nothing. The spectacle of ubiquitous war leaves man's future in doubt. Let us now examine the atheistic forces of Masonry and Marxism. After fifty years of Marxism, let us ask what their achievements have been. They held the destiny of the world in their hands and dominated the fate of nations. What have they left us? They have bequeathed something other than peace and justice. They brought the world to the brink of nuclear and ecological catastrophe. They have left us a world plagued by wars. They created a system in which the few exploited the masses. Here, dear Benson, we must disagree with you.

The godless powers which sought to resolve all man's problems have left us nothing but bankruptcy. The new world order set out to erase God and the Catholic Church. The Catholic Church and the papacy are the real moral authority in this gigantic struggle, which fought strenuously for peace, true justice, and authentic defense of human rights. Clinging to the affirmation of the transcendent and to the relationship between creature and Creator, the Catholic Church is able to make sense of man's life, his suffering, and his death. She is also able to defend the demands of peace and true justice.

We cannot know the future. However, we can perceive a conflict between the so-called "world order," based on power, and the Catholic Church under the papacy which it treats as an enemy to be overcome and an obstacle to progress in the world. Benson rightly perceived this. Certainly we live in an era in which political and economic forces no longer support the Church. Quite the contrary. These are times in which political and economic forces are impatient with the Church because she wishes to remain true to herself.

Will there be persecution, dear friends? There will be persecution and seduction.

The Christians who will embrace the "sacrament of euthanasia" in the new world order will be most welcome in the society of the future. They will believe in the seduction of modern times and they will strive to kill the faith and the Church. Those who remain faithful to Christ will be persecuted. Benson warns us clearly about this persecution and admonishes us to prepare for it.

Weapons for the "Good Fight"

Now we must examine the reaction of the Church and of Christians to the "great religious deception" which will explode at the end of time, but which is latent in every age. We should not forget this last point.

With what weapons must the Christian arm himself for the "good fight" at the end of time—the time of great deception and of the great persecution of the Church—which is Satan's last attempt to take man away from God? Arms are necessary in all ages, but at the end of time they become decisive.

This is a theme which concerns us immediately, and we shall approach it in the light of Benson's novel, which is imbued with a prophetic wisdom distilled from his intense mysticism.

Fidelity to the Pope

At the time of the Antichrist, world powers will be divided into two opposing camps. Instead of Christ, the human race will accept the new progressive and deifying religion headed by him who is "savior," "redeemer," and "lord" of the world, who will be the glorious fruit of mankind—the Antichrist. A small group of strict Catholics will stand by the Pope. Strangely, in Benson's outlook no mention is made of any other religions. Unlike Soloviev, there is no reference to any little groups of Protestants or Orthodox. In Benson's novel, only the Pope and a few remaining Catholics are not assimilated into humanitarianism. Only the "little flock" headed by Peter will remain faithful. I believe that one of the most striking and instructive points raised by the book is that the greater the Antichrist's and Satan's power of seduction, the greater the false splendor of human progress. In those times nobody will be able to resist the seduction except those whom we have already mentioned. "Thou art Peter, and upon this rock I will build my Church, and the gates of hell shall not prevail against it" (Matt. 16:18, Douay-Rheims). This is Benson's exegesis of the words of Christ as contained in St. Matthew's Gospel. Times will come, says Benson, the end times, in which no one will be able to preserve the faith unless they cling to the rock of Peter, the Pope, on which Christ built his Church. Only those in the Catholic Church who cling to the rock, against which the waves of evil break, will be able to preserve the faith. All others will be seduced. All others will be annexed to the new religion. This has profound theological significance. According to Benson, the battles will not be "religions" drawn up on one side of the field and "humanitarianism" on the other. Rather, the Catholic Church will be reduced to a little flock while all the other religions will be arrayed against it. The non-Christian religions and the non-Catholic Christian confessions will be absorbed immediately and unified by the principle of naturalism, unless they return to the common house that is the Catholic Church.

This is a prophetic vision of the papacy. I believe that it is being confirmed by the events of the times in which we live. Today the papacy represents the supernatural principle. The Pope's authority opposes what is promoted by today's world, everything that is contrary to God, everything that is contrary to the moral law. The papacy is set against the world, insofar as the world is dominated by the spirit of the world. Who dares to oppose humanitarian religion? Who dares to affirm the moral law that is above man and guides him? Who challenges those who wish to govern the world without God or set up a government superior to God? Among the religions of the world today, who has the courage to challenge the global authority of those who cherish a vision of the world in which religion, where it exists, honors the Antichrist and is at his service?

Friends, in today's world, apart from the Pope, is there any religious authority which can say "no," with strength and courage, to man's pretensions to master his own destiny? No such authority is to be seen.

In Benson's vision, the two antagonists of the future are Julian Felsenburgh, the Antichrist, and a little English priest, Fr. Percy, who will be elected the last pope and take the name Silvester. The final reckoning, the conclusion of history, will be worked out between these two protagonists, who represent the eternal protagonists of the infernal dragon and of Christ. Humanity will be divided between one or other of them and regrouped around this or that principle, this or that representative. History will end in conflict. This vision has all the characteristics of prophecy. The prince of this world, incarnate in the Antichrist, will be strenuously opposed by the Pope, the Roman pontiff.

In some very outstanding pages, Benson outlines the program and the initiatives mounted by the penultimate Pope against the rising tide of the times of the Antichrist. The entire world, however, has become directly subject to Felsenburgh's political domination. The *pastor angelicus*, the penultimate pope, arrives at an agreement with the government whereby his sovereignty over the entire city of Rome is recognized in exchange for the all the churches of Italy, which are ceded to the temporal authorities. Insensible to world public opinion, part of his program of silent, but strenuous, resistance to the apostasy includes giving Rome a very particular form of public administration. Its object is to maintain supernatural values and to insist on the importance of exclusive and unique eternal salvation. While the political domination of the Antichrist extends throughout the whole world, Christians who identify with the Pope's program pour into Rome and, together with the Pope, prepare to face the time of the great deception.

> [He] had since set himself to make it a city of saints. He had cared, it appeared, nothing whatever for the world's opinion: his policy, so far as it could be called one, consisted in a very simple thing; he had declared in Epistle after Epistle that the object of the Church was to do glory to God by producing supernatural virtues in man and that nothing at all was of any significance or importance except so far as it effected this object.

Benson's critique is directed here against progressive humanitarian Christianity which has forgotten the supernatural objective for which the Church was founded—the glory of God and the salvation of souls—so as to confirm the world in its ideals.

> He had further maintained that since Peter was the rock, the City of Peter was the capital of the world, and should set an example to its dependency: this could not be done unless Peter rule his City; and therefore he had sacrificed every church and ecclesiastical building in the country for that one end. Then he set about ruling his city:... he had said that, on the whole, the latter-day discoveries of man tended to distract immortal souls from a contemplation of eternal verities—not that these discoveries could be anything but good in themselves, since after all they gave insight into the wonderful laws of God—but that at present they were too exciting to the imagination. So he removed the trams, the volors, the laboratories, the manufactories—saying that

there was plenty of room for them outside Rome—and had allowed them to be planted in the suburbs: in their place he had raised shrines, religious houses and Calvaries.

Here Benson speaks in paradox but underlines the great truth that man needs only one thing—the salvation of his soul (cf. Luke 10:42). The Pope restored the city so as continually to remind man of this truth. He desired that every distraction of luxury be removed from the city.

> Then he had attended further to the souls of his subjects. Since Rome was of limited area, and still more because the world corrupted without its proper salt, he allowed no man under the age of fifty to live within its walls for more than one month in each year, except those who received his permit: They might live, of course, immediately outside the city (and they did, by tens of thousands).

Many may laugh at this scenario, but Benson gives expression to a profound truth: woe to the Church should she conform to the world. What is salt worth if it should lose its saltiness? What use is a lamp if placed under a bushel? What value has yeast should it not have the capacity to leaven dough? The object of the penultimate pope, in the midst of a naturalistic sea, was to preserve supernatural principle in its integrity; to keep the flame burning in the time of the great flood and to carry it on after the flood.

> Freemasonry was steadily denounced.... Men were urged to remember their immortal souls and the Majesty of God, and to reflect upon the fact that in a few years all would be called to give their account to Him who was creator and Ruler of the world.... That was the line of action which took the world completely by surprise. People had expected

hysteria, argument and passionate exhortation: disguised emissaries, plots and protests. There were none of these. It was as if progress had not yet begun, and volors were uninvented, as if the entire universe had not come to disbelieve in God. Here was this silly old man, talking in his sleep, babbling of the Cross, and the inner life, and the forgiveness of sins, exactly as his predecessors had talked for two thousand years before. Well, it was only one sign more that Rome had lost not only its power, but its common sense as well. It was really time that something should be done.

Benson's first warning to the Christians of the end times was that only the "little flock" would conserve the faith and these would be close to the Pope, the Vicar of Christ, the rock against which the gates of Hell will not prevail. Hence the importance of absolute fidelity to the papacy. Ultimately this implies faith in the presence of Christ in his Church, and in a special way in the Pope, "sweet Christ on earth." Such fidelity is a reaffirmation of the supernatural principle.

Prayer

Prayer is another fundamental weapon for the great battle of the end times. When man will glorify himself and proclaim the Antichrist as God made man, the supernatural principle will be preserved only by those who cling to the divine presence in prayer. These will "experience" God, His existence, lordship, power, and glory. In the time of the Antichrist, the power of suggestion will cloud reason. Only those who intimately experience the supernatural in prayer will have the strength to acknowledge God's existence, despite the apparent evidence to the contrary. How, dear friends, can we reason with a world which does not believe? How do we dialogue with a world which regards faith as auto-suggestion? How do we impress a world that asserts "you are wrong, there is no God, stop dreaming"? What do we say to those who regard Catholics as a group of imbeciles surrounding an old man, the Pope? In such times, what reasons can be given for believing? If you can think of no other reason, then might you perhaps begin to think that you are wrong and that others are right?

Thus, in an era marked by the seduction of the heart, of a general obscuring of the mind, and of the folly of reason, only those who have had a strong experience of God in prayer will preserve the faith. In that supernatural experience, the faith will be conserved, and you will conform to it. If you look to the sun and see the light, even if man denies the existence of the sun, what can you say? Having seen the sun, you will not vacillate in the faith. You will be a rock in the waves of the sea.

Benson develops this theme at several points in his novel. What he has to say about prayer is obviously nourished by his own personal experience, while presenting the most important character in the novel—Fr. Percy, an English priest who becomes the last pope and takes the name Silvester. He is Julian Felsenburgh's antagonist. He must overcome the seduction of the world and the Antichrist to become pope. He must overcome the seductions of the end times. He accomplishes this through prayer, which is self-immersion in God so as to touch Him in the dimness of faith and to surrender oneself in total self-giving to God, trusting absolutely in Him.

Those who do not have this faith—the only true faith—and this prayer—the only true prayer—will succumb to the universal temptation. This is the theme of the dramatic colloquium between Fr. Percy and another priest, Fr. Francis. Like many other priests and ordinary Christians, Fr. Francis believes that the faith is a pure auto-suggestion. He leaves the Church.

In this episode, Benson insists that prayer alone emerges victorious from the terrible temptations of the end times. Fr. Francis has experienced a deep crisis. He is intimately aware of defeat. He decides to abandon the fight and renounce the Church.

"It is an end of everything," said the other ... in a perfectly steady voice. "I believe nothing. I have believed nothing for a year now."

"You have felt nothing, you mean," said Percy.

"That won't do, father," went on the other. "I tell you, there is nothing left. I can't even argue now. It is just good-bye."

Percy had nothing to say. He had talked to this man during a period of over eight months, ever since Father Francis had first confided in him that his faith was going. He understood perfectly what a strain it had been: he felt bitterly compassionate towards this poor creature who had become caught up somehow into the dizzy triumphant whirl of the New Humanity. External facts were horribly strong just now; and faith, except to one who had learned that Will and Grace were all and emotion nothing, was as a child crawling about in the midst of some huge machinery: it might survive or it might not; but it required nerves of steel to keep steady. It was hard to know where blame could be assigned; yet Percy's faith told him that there was blame due. In the ages of faith a very inadequate grasp of religion would pass muster; in these searching days none but the humble and the pure could stand the test for long, unless indeed they were protected by a miracle of ignorance. [Blessed be the ignorant, dear friends.] The alliance of Psychology and Materialism did indeed seem,

looked at from one angle, to account for everything; it
needed a robust supernatural perception to understand
their practical inadequacy. And as regards Father Francis's
personal responsibility, he could not help feeling that the
other had allowed ceremonial to play too great a part in
his religion, and prayer too little. In him the external had
absorbed the internal.

Fr. Percy tries to move his friend from his position of pride,
but words prove futile.

"Listen to me. You can say Christianity is absurd and impossible. Now, you know, it cannot be that! It may be untrue – I
am not speaking of that now, even though I am perfectly
certain that it is absolutely true – but it cannot be absurd
so long as educated and virtuous people continue to hold
it. To say that it is absurd is simple pride; it is to dismiss all
who believe in it as not merely mistaken but as unintelligent
as well ... you still really believe it to be absurd: you have
told me so a dozen times. Well, I repeat, that is pride and
quite sufficient to account for it all."

In the bitterness of his lack of humility, Fr. Francis rejects Fr.
Percy's efforts to help him:

There was silence for a moment after that. Percy had really
no more to say. He had talked to him of the inner life again
and again, in which verities are seen to be true, and acts
of faith are ratified; he had urged prayer and humility till
he was almost weary of the names; and he had been met
by the retort that this was to advise sheer self-hypnotism;
and he had despaired of making clear to one who did not
see it for himself that while Love and Faith may be called

self-hypnotism from one angle, yet from another they are as much realities as, for example, artistic faculties, and need similar cultivation; that they produce a conviction that they are convictions; that they handle and taste things which when handled and tasted are overwhelmingly more real and objective than the things of sense. Evidences seemed to mean nothing to this man. So he was silent now, chilled himself by the presence of this crisis, looking unseeingly out upon the plain, little old-world parlor, its tall window, its strip of matting, conscious chiefly of the dreary hopeless-ness of this human brother of his who had eyes but did not see, ears and was deaf.

To his brother, sitting there obstinate in his bitter decision, Fr. Percy stated clearly:

"I am only terribly sorry. You see I know that it's all true."

The other looked at him heavily.

"And I know that it is not … it is very beautiful; I wish I could believe it. I don't think I shall be ever happy again—but—but there it is."

Percy sighed. He had told him so often that the heart is as divine a gift as the mind, and that to neglect it in the search for God is to seek ruin, but this priest had scarcely seen the application to himself. He had answered with the old psychological arguments that the suggestions of educa-tion accounted for everything.

In the time of the great trial those who have not experienced God in faith and prayer will indeed believe that psychology—the world —is right when it holds that the faith is auto-suggestion. Having spoken with his friend who betrays the faith, Fr. Percy recollects himself in prayer. Fr. Francis, like Judas, goes out into the darkness. In a beautiful passage, Benson shows how Fr. Percy's faith emerges from prayer invigored and renewed:

> He drew a couple of long breaths and set to work.... There on the left shone the refracted glow of the lamps that burned before the Lord in the Sacrament, on the right a dozen candles winked here and there at the foot of the gaunt images, high overhead hung the gigantic cross with that lean, emaciated Poor Man Who called all who looked on Him to the embraces of God. Then he hid his hands, drew a couple of breaths and set to work.
>
> He began, as his custom was in mental prayer, by a deliberate act of self-exclusion from the world of sense. Under the image of sinking beneath a surface he forced himself downwards and inwards, till the peal of the organ, the shuffle of footsteps, the rigidity of the chair-back beneath his wrists—all seemed apart and external, and he was left a single person with a beating heart, an intellect that suggested image after image, and emotions that were too languid to stir themselves. Then he made his second descent, renounced all that he possessed and was, and became conscious that even the body was left behind and that his mind and heart, awed by the Presence in which they found themselves, clung close and obedient to the will which was their lord and protector. He drew another long breath, or two, and felt that Presence surge about him; he repeated a few mechanical words, and sank to that peace which follows the relinquishment of thought.... He was within the veil of things now, beyond the barriers of sense and reflection, in that secret place to which he had learned

the road by endless effort, in that strange region where realities are evident, where perceptions go to and fro with the swiftness of light, where the swaying will catches now this, now that act, molds it and speeds it; where all things meet, where truth is known and handled and tasted, where God Immanent is one with God Transcendent, where the meaning of the external world is evident through its inner side, and the Church and its mysteries are seen from within a haze of glory.

So he lay a few moments, absorbing and resting. Then he aroused himself to consciousness and began to speak.

"Lord, I am here and Thou art here. I know Thee. There is nothing else but Thou and I.... I lay this all in Thy hands—Thy apostate priest, Thy people, the world, and myself. I spread it before Thee.... Myself, Lord—there but for Thy grace should I be going, in darkness and misery. It is Thou Who dost preserve me. Maintain and finish Thy work within my soul. Let me not falter for one instant."

So his soul stood a moment, with outstretched appealing hands, helpless and confident. Then the will flickered in self-consciousness, and he repeated acts of faith, hope and love to steady it. Then he drew another long breath, feeling the Presence tingle and shake about him, and began again.

"Lord, look on Thy people. Many are falling from Thee. *Ne in aeternum irascaris nobis....* I unite myself with all Thy saints and angels and Mary Queen of Heaven; look on them and me, and hear us. *Emitte lucem tuam et veritatem tuam.* Thy light and Thy truth! Lay not on us heavier burdens than we can bear. Lord, why dost Thou not speak?"

He writhed himself forward in a passion of expectant desire, hearing his muscles crack in the effort. Once more he relaxed himself; and the swift play of wordless acts began which he knew to be the very heart of prayer. The eyes of his soul flew hither and thither, from Calvary to Heaven and back again to the tossing troubled earth. He saw Christ dying of desolation while the earth rocked and groaned; Christ reigning as priest upon His Throne in robes of light; Christ patient and inexorably silent within the Sacramental species; and to each in turn he directed the eyes of the Eternal Father....

Then he waited for communications, and they came, so soft and delicate, passing tike shadows, that his will sweated blood and tears in the effort to catch and fix them and correspond....

He saw the Body Mystical in its agony, strained over the world as on a cross, silent with pain; he saw this and that nerve wrenched and twisted, till pain presented it to himself as under the guise of flashes of color; he saw the life-blood drop by drop run down from His head and hands and feet. The world was gathered mocking and good-humored beneath.... Far away, behind bushes and in holes of the ground the friends of Jesus peeped and sobbed; Mary herself was silent, pierced by seven swords; the disciple whom He loved had no words of comfort.

He saw, too, how no word would be spoken from heaven; the angels themselves were bidden to put sword into sheath, and wait on the eternal patience of God, for the agony was hardly yet begun; there were a thousand horrors yet before the end could come, that final sum of crucifixion.... He must wait and watch, content to stand there and do nothing; and the Resurrection must seem to him no more than a dreamed-of hope. There was the

Sabbath yet to come, while the Body Mystical [the Church] must lie in its sepulchre cut off from light, and even the dignity of the Cross must be withdrawn and the knowledge that Jesus lived. That inner world, to which by long effort he had learned the way, was all alight with agony; it was bitter as brine, it was of that pale luminosity that is the utmost product of pain, it hummed in his ears with a note that rose to a scream ... it pressed upon him, penetrated him, stretched him as on a rack.... And with that his will grew sick and nerveless.

"Lord, I cannot bear it!" he moaned.

This, dear friends, is the kind of prayer that will bring the Church of the end times to contemplate the passion. It will be our true strength to overcome the trial of trials.

Willingness to Accept Martyrdom

Christians in the end times will be reduced to a "little flock." In resisting seduction and persecution, they will have to employ the weapon of unity with the Pope who is the rock, and above all else the supernatural weapon of prayer.

In Benson's view, another disposition is absolutely indispensable for Christians at the end of time. Reflecting a perfectly accurate reading of the eleventh chapter of Revelation, which speaks of the two witnesses who gave their lives for the faith, Benson recommends generous willingness to bear witness to the faith to the point of martyrdom. The end times will be similar to the beginning. The little flock will be formed of Christians as meek as lambs and as brave as lions—similar to Him who is called the Lion of Judah. They will willingly give their lives for the faith and for the Church.

The Wrath of God

In the end times, Benson imagines that the Pope will institute the most important religious order in the history of Christianity. It will surpass all other religious orders. The Pope himself will be a member. Bishops and cardinals, and especially the faithful, will be called to join it. It will be the order of Christ Crucified and its members will be willing to shed their blood as a supreme witness for the faith.

The idea of a new order was born in Fr. Percy's heart. In colloquy with the penultimate pope—who was killed together with the cardinals during the Antichrist's bombardment of Rome—Fr. Percy, a young priest (the same age as Felsenburgh, thirty-three), gave his analysis and evaluation of the terrible crisis facing the Church and of the fact that nobody yet realized that the end times were at hand:

> It was the intention of God and His Vicars to reconcile all men in Christ Jesus; but the corner-stone had once more been rejected, and instead of the chaos that the pious had prophesied, there was coming into existence a unity unlike anything known in history. This was the more deadly from the fact that it contained so many elements of indubitable good. War, apparently, was now extinct, and it was not Christianity that had done it; union was now seen to be better than disunion, and the lesson had been learned apart from the Church. In fact, natural virtues had suddenly waxed luxuriant, [of a sudden all were honest, good, and generous] and supernatural virtues were despised. Friendliness took the place of charity, contentment the place of hope, and knowledge the place of faith.

Percy continues his description and outlines the dangerous character of Julian Felsenburgh, who would manifest himself as the

Antichrist. He came from the United States, home of that un-limited confidence in human nature and its virtues. His worldly success is indicative of the fact that he is the perfect incarnation of the spirit pervading the age:

> He had accomplished a work that—apart from God—seemed miraculous.... He had prevailed by sheer force of personality over the two supreme tyrants of life—religious fanaticism and party government.

In the eyes of the multitude and of public opinion, his personality has assumed religious connotations:

> Percy here described one or two of his little scenes, saying that it was like the vision of a god: and he quoted freely some of the titles given to the Man by sober, unhysterical newspapers. Felsenburgh was called the Son of Man, because he was so pure-bred a cosmopolitan; the Savior of the World, because he had slain war and himself survived—even—even—here Percy's voice faltered—even Incarnate God, because he was the perfect representative of divine man.

Fr. Percy expresses his conviction that Catholics, because of the irreconcilability of their notion of the transcendent with the spirit of the world, would soon face persecution:

> Persecution, he said, was coming. There had been a riot or two already. But persecution was not to be feared. It would no doubt cause apostasies, as it had always done, but these were deplorable only on account of the individual apostates. On the other hand, it would reassure the faithful; and purge out the half-hearted. Once, in the early ages,

Satan's attack had been made on the bodily side, with whips and fire and beasts; ... in the twentieth century [it would be made] on the springs of moral and spiritual life. Now it seemed as if the assault was on all three planes at once. But what was chiefly to be feared was the positive influence of Humanitarianism: it was coming, like the Kingdom of God, with power; it was crushing the imaginative and the romantic, it was assuming rather than asserting its own truth; it was smothering with bolsters instead of wounding and stimulating with steel or controversy. It seemed to be forcing its way, almost objectively, into the inner world.

Percy had grasped the difficulty of the age. He understood its capacity radically to seduce man's heart, mind and body. He continues his analysis and predictions:

Persons who had scarcely heard its [Humanitarianism's] name were professing its tenets; priests absorbed it, as they absorbed God in Communion—he mentioned the names of the recent apostates—children drank it in like Christianity itself. The soul "naturally Christian" seemed to be becoming "the soul naturally infidel." Persecution, cried the priest, was to be welcomed like salvation, prayed for, and grasped; but he feared that the authorities were too shrewd, and knew the antidote and the poison apart.

They would persecute Catholics to enter their ranks: "There might be individual martyrdoms—in fact, there would be, and very many, but they would be in spite of secular government, not because of it." Finally, the humanitarians "would presently put on the dress of liturgy and sacrifice" so as to deceive all, "and when that was done, the Church's cause, unless God intervened, would be over."

With paternal tenderness, the aged pope asks the young priest who has understood the dangers and deceptions of the times with the insight of faith what can be done. Fr. Percy replies:

"Holy Father—the Mass, prayer, the Rosary. These first and last. The world denies their power: it is on their power that Christians must throw all their weight. All things in Jesus Christ—in Jesus Christ, first and last. Nothing else can avail. He must do all, for we can do nothing."

Then he adds, at once audaciously and hesitantly:

"Holiness ... I have an old scheme ... every fool has desired it: a new Order, Holiness—a new Order ... no habit or badge—subject to Your Holiness only, freer than Jesuits, poorer than Franciscans, more mortified than Carthusians: men and women alike—the three vows with the intention of martyrdom;... Holiness, it is the thought of a fool ... and Christ Crucified for their patron."

The Pope stood up abruptly ... [and] extending his hand, [said] "God bless you, my son."

As we have already seen, the old Pope would die in the bombing of Rome. Fr. Percy would be his successor. The Pope of the end times approved the project placed before him by the young priest and founded the new religious Order of Christ Crucified. It had the traditional vows. To these would be added a fourth which distinguished it from all other orders—a vow of martyrdom which involved bearing witness to the faith unto death. Preparations were now made to face the wave, indeed the inundation, of the Antichrist. Addressing the College of Cardinals, the Pope described the peculiarities of the new order by referring to many religious orders which had been founded during the course of history:

Each (religious order) was raised up at a particular season of need, and each had corresponded nobly with the divine vocation.... At this present season then, it appears to Our Humility that all such orders (which once more We commend and bless) are not perfectly suited by the very conditions of their respective rules to perform the great work which the time requires. Our warfare lies not with ignorance in particular, whether of the heathens to whom the Gospel has not yet come, or of those whose fathers have rejected it, nor with the deceitful riches of the world, nor with science falsely so-called, nor indeed with any of those strongholds of infidelity against whom We have labored in the past. Rather, it appears as if at last the time was come of which the Apostle spoke when he said that "that day shall not come, except there come a falling away first, and that Man of Sin be revealed, the Son of Perdition, who opposeth and exalteth himself above all that is called God." It is not with this or that force that we are concerned, but rather with the unveiled immensity of that power whose time was foretold, and whose destruction is prepared [the power of the Antichrist].

It seems good, then, to Our Humility, that the Vicar of Christ should himself invite God's children to this new warfare; and it is our intention to enroll under the title of the Order of Christ Crucified the names of all who offer themselves to this supreme service. In doing this We are aware of the novelty of Our action, and the disregard of all such precautions as have been necessary in the past. We take counsel in this matter with none save Him Who we believe has inspired it.

First, then, let Us say, that although obedient service will be required from all who shall be admitted to this Order, our primary intention in instituting it lies in God's regard rather than in man's, in appealing to Him Who asks our generosity rather than to those who deny it, and dedicating once more by a formal and deliberate act our soul and bodies to the heavenly Will and service of Him Who alone can rightly claim such offering, and will accept our poverty.

Briefly we dictate only the following conditions: None shall be capable of entering the Order except such as shall be above the age of seventeen years. No badge, habit, or insignia shall be attached to it. The three Evangelical Counsels shall be the foundation of the Rule, to which we add a fourth intention, namely, that of desire to receive the crown of martyrdom and a purpose of embracing it. The bishop of every diocese, if he himself shall enter the Order, shall be the superior within the limits of his own jurisdiction, and alone shall be exempt from the literal observance of the vow of poverty so long as he retains his see.... We announce Our intention of Ourself entering the Order as its supreme prelate, and of making Our profession within the course of a few days.

Having clarified the specific functions of the new order and outlined some of the particular norms for the regulation of its life, the Pope concluded:

It is Our wish that these words shall be communicated to all the world, that there may be no delay in making known what it is that Christ through His Vicar asks of all who profess the Divine Name. We offer no rewards except those which God Himself has promised to those that love Him, and lay down their life for Him; no promise of peace, save of that which passeth understanding; no home save that which befits pilgrims and sojourners who seek a City to come; no honor save the world's contempt; no life, save that which is hid with Christ in God.

Dear friends, we do not know whether we are already in these times, the end times, of which Benson speaks. Reading these pages, however, we immediately realize one thing: the age of opportunistic Christianity has passed; the age of comfortable Christianity has gone; the age of arm-chair militancy is at an end. We live in heroic times, time of heroic witness—to be Christian today means rowing against the tide. Conserving the faith implies struggling against seduction. We live in an age in which those who resist must be prepared to face martyrdom.

While we do not know whether these are the end times, it is clear that we live in times in which Christianity is more similar to its origins. Every Christian is called to be a David, ready to fight the Goliath who will try to destroy the faith and the Church.

Benson demands a militant Christianity—even if the Church is reduced to a tiny flock—with the faithful vowed to martyrdom. This very demand was prophesied by one of the great Marian writers, St. Louis-Marie Grignion de Montfort.

Mary and the End Times

At this point, it would be appropriate to consider Mary's role in the end times. Benson speaks of apparitions of Our Lady to a group of children in Ireland as the world lies under the Antichrist's dominion. Soloviev concludes his *Tale* with the apparition of the "woman clothed with the sun" who precedes the final coming of Christ, just as the Antichrist completes his attempt to become lord of the world.

It is interesting that Soloviev and Benson should concentrate on Mary's protection of the Church in the final battle—a theme amply explored by St. Louis Marie Grignion de Montfort. This great theme is well-established in Scripture and has profound theological significance. The latter times will be characterized by Lucifer's assault on the Church and his efforts to destroy it. It is only normal and theologically consistent to suggest that Mary would be at her most vigilant in these times, sustaining the Church, the Pope, and all the faithful in their final victory in which they will crush the head of the serpent with her.

In the end times, Christ will come in victory and the Blessed Virgin Mary will crush the head of the serpent. As Christ's first coming was prepared by Mary, so shall his second coming in triumph be prepared and activated by Mary. This is the theological motivation for the role of Mary in the latter days found in the writings of Benson, Soloviev, and St. Louis de Montfort.

I should also like to point out the connection between Benson's intuition of an "Order of Christ Crucified" and that of St. Louis de Montfort, who sees at the end times a militant force of Mary's children.

Benson's Order of Christ Crucified, with its votaries dedicated to the witness of martyrdom, much resembles the children of Mary who have been chosen by her to resist the seduction of the Evil One and Antichrist's determination to eradicate the faith. Together with Mary, they will crush the head of the serpent and bring about Christ's victorious coming.

The *Treatise on True Devotion to the Blessed Virgin*[20] contains a Marian form of Benson's intuition. The end times will have their own special apostles, headed by the Pope and including cardinals,

---

[20] *True Devotion to the Blessed Virgin*, in *God Alone: The Collected Writings of St. Louis-Marie de Montfort* (Bay Shore, NY: Montfort Publications, 1987), 289–397.

bishops, religious, and laity. These will be vowed to martyrdom. The apostles of the end times will be Marian:

> But Mary's power over the evil spirits will especially shine forth in the latter times, when Satan will lie in wait for her heel, that is, for her humble servants and poor children whom she will rouse to fight against him. In the eyes of the world they will be little and poor, and like the heel, lowly in the eyes of all, down-trodden and crushed as is the heel by the other parts of the body. But in compensation for this they will be rich in God's graces, which will be abundantly bestowed on them by Mary. They will be great and exalted before God in holiness. They will be superior to all creatures by their great zeal and so strongly will they be supported by divine assistance that, in union with Mary, they will crush the head of Satan with their heel, that is, their humility and bring victory to Jesus Christ.

De Montfort asks: "But what will they be like, these servants, these slaves, these children of Mary?" He replies:

> They will be ministers of the Lord who, like a flaming fire, will enkindle everywhere the fires of divine love. They will become, in Mary's powerful hands, like sharp arrows, with which she will transfix her enemies. They will be as the children of Levi, thoroughly purified by the fire of great tribulations and closely joined to God. They will carry the gold of love in their heart, the frankincense of prayer in their mind and the myrrh of mortification in their body. They will bring to the poor and lowly everywhere the sweet fragrance of Jesus, but they will bring the odor of death to the great, the rich and the proud of this world. They will be like thunder-clouds

flying through the air at the slightest breath of the Holy Spirit. Attached to nothing, surprised by nothing, troubled at nothing, they will shower down the rain of God's word and of eternal life. They will thunder against sin, they will storm against the world, they will strike down the devil and his followers and for life and for death, they will pierce through and through with the two-edged sword of God's word all those against whom they are sent by Almighty God. They will be true apostles of the latter times to whom the Lord of Hosts will give eloquence and strength to work wonders and carry off glorious spoils from His enemies. They will sleep without gold or silver and, more important still, without concern in the midst of other priests, ecclesiastics and clerics. Yet they will have the silver wings of the dove enabling them to go wherever the Holy Spirit calls them, filled as they are with the resolve to seek the glory of God and the salvation of souls. Wherever they preach, they will leave behind them nothing but the gold of love, which is the fulfillment of the whole law. Lastly, we know they will be true disciples of Jesus Christ, imitating His poverty, His humility, His contempt of the world and His love. They will point out the narrow way to God in pure truth according to the holy Gospel, and not according to the maxims of the world. Their hearts will not be troubled, nor will they show favor to anyone; they will not spare or heed or fear any man, however powerful he may be.

Dear friends, I regard the present Pope, John Paul II, as one of these apostles. Who does not? St. Louis-Marie Grignion de Montfort continues:

They will have the two-edged sword of the Word of God in their mouths and the blood-stained standard of the Cross on their shoulders. They will carry the crucifix in their right hand and the rosary in their left, and the holy names of Jesus and Mary on their heart. The simplicity and self-sacrifice of Jesus will be reflected in their whole behavior. Such are the great men who are to come. By the will of God Mary is to prepare them to extend His rule over the impious and unbelievers. But when and how will this come about? Only God knows. For our part we must yearn and wait for it in silence and in prayer.

Are we perhaps living in these times? Are these the times of the great apostles of Mary, of the Order of Christ Crucified? We do not know. Certainly this century is under the protection of Mary; we live in the time of Mary. Are the times of Mary the end times? It is difficult to say.

Epilogue

We have come, dear friends, to the epilogue of Benson's novel. As we have seen, the squadrons of the Antichrist have destroyed Rome. Percy Franklin was created cardinal. He and two other cardinals are all that remain of the Sacred College. The College of Cardinals, the last pope, and nearly all Catholics have been killed in the bombing of Rome. Percy, by two votes to one, is elected the last pope and takes the name of Silvester. After the destruction of the city, disguised as a Bedouin, he takes refuge in Nazareth. From there he tries to guide the few remaining Catholics scattered throughout the world. Thanks to the Order of Christ Crucified, he succeeds in providing the Church with a skeleton administration in spite of the reduced number of clergy and faithful. On the very day of the promulgation of the "Law of Atheism," he is betrayed by one of twelve cardinals created by him. He is discovered. Once informed that there is still a pope and a Church, the Antichrist decides to eradicate the superstition once and for all. Together with the powerful of this world, he determines to eliminate Catholicism. In a symbolic gesture his spokesman announces:

> "His Honor's proposal is ... that a force should proceed during the night of Saturday next to Palestine, and on the Sunday morning, when these men will be all gathered together, that this force should finish as swiftly and mercifully as possible the work to which the Powers have set their hands. So far, the consent of the governments which have been consulted has been unanimous, and there is little doubt that the rest will be equally so. His Honor felt that he could not act in so grave a matter on His own responsibility; it is not merely local; it is a catholic administration of justice, and will have results wider than it is safe minutely to prophesy.... Each government, it is proposed, should take part in the final scene, for it is something of a symbolic action; and for this purpose it is thought well that each of the three Departments of the World should depute volors, to the number of the constituting states, one hundred and twenty-two all told, to set about the business.... The rendezvous, then, should be no other than Nazareth itself."

This is the Armageddon. Through his secretary, Felsenburgh continues:

> "With respect to the exact method of carrying out the conclusion, His Honor is inclined to think that it will be more merciful to enter into no negotiations with the persons concerned. An opportunity should be given to the inhabitants of the village to make their escape if they

so desire it, and then, with the explosives that the force should carry, the end can be practically instantaneous. For Himself, His Honor proposes to be there in person, and further that the actual discharge should take place from His own car. It seems but suitable that the world which has done His Honor the goodness to elect Him to its President-ship should act through His hands; and this would be at least some slight token of respect to a superstition which, however infamous, is yet the one and only force capable of withstanding the true progress of man. His Honor promises … that in the event of this plan being carried out, we shall be no more troubled by Christianity."

While the world, dear friends, is convinced that it has finished with Christianity and with the last tiny flock of Christians, Silvester prepares to celebrate the final Mass with his followers in the little house in Nazareth. He contemplates the Host in adoration. At that very moment the forces of the Antichrist draw closer to Nazareth to destroy the Catholic Church. During the singing of the "Pange lingua," Percy Franklin has a vision in which there appears to him in a ray of supernatural light:

the heir of temporal ages and the Exile of eternity, the final piteous Prince of Rebels, the creature against God, blinder than the sun which paled and the earth that shook; and, as He came, passing even through the last material stage to the thinness of a spirit-fabric, the floating circle swirled behind Him, tossing like phantom birds in the wake of a phantom ship…. He was coming, and the earth, rent once again in its allegiance, shrank and reeled in the agony of divided homage. He was coming.

Christ, the true Lord of the World.

Is It the End of the World?

Having reached the end of this great, suggestive, and instructive fresco, we conclude by offering some doctrinal principles to assist in discerning wisely a moment in history marked by revelations of dubious doctrine, uncertain in provenance and capable of leading people astray. The rigorous Christian avoids every superficial attitude which neglects the aspect of waiting which characterizes Christian faith and nourishes an attitude of hope with regard to the future. He does not indulge in the terrifying obsession with cataclysm so typical of the sects.

We have already said much about the Catholic vision of the end of the world. Here we will synthesize the principal elements of that doctrine as drawn from the Church's reflection on the Word of God. The Church has always meditated on the end of time and, from the outset, has proposed sure teaching so as to help the faithful read the future through the eyes of faith.

Have the End Times Begun?

Before anything else, it is necessary to understand the period of history in which we live. Christians read history through the eyes of faith. The history of the world and of man is the actualization of God's plan. The world, St. Paul tells us several times in his letters, was created not only by the Word but also with a view to the Word. In synthesis, we can say that the world and man were created with a view to the Incarnation, which comes about with a view to man's redemption and glorification in Christ. History reaches fulfillment when Christ, as judge, consigns a redeemed world to the Father so that "God may be all in all" (1 Cor. 15:28).

Faith sees in the history of the world, and of man, the unfolding of a great plan of love which is stronger than the error, confusion, and perversion to which human liberty can become enslaved. This optimistic outlook, based on the triumph of superabundant grace over sin, must continually inform the believer's view of reality, especially when the power of evil seems invincible or eternal death a concrete threat bearing down on life.

We are in the final stage of the unfolding of God's marvelous plan. This phase runs from the Ascension of Christ into Heaven all the way to His return in glory to judge the living and the dead, thereby ending human history. Once the work of redemption was accomplished in Jesus Christ, the time for the distribution of the fruits of that redemption to man began. Since this is the final phase of the history of salvation, we can say that we live in the end times, which encompass the period between Christ's first and His final coming. After this time, there will be no other. With the coming of Christ in glory time will end and eternity will begin. It will be an eternity of happiness with God for those who accepted Him in this life. Those who rejected Him in this life and who have not repented will be engulfed by eternal death.

In highlighting this undoubted aspect of the faith, that we are living in the final phase of human history, we must try to understand all the characteristics of this period during which God has brought us into being.

Christ Is Lord of the Last Days

An important characteristic of the final phase of human history is the fact that Christ is its head and Lord. Before the accomplishment of our redemption, the world, by divine disposition, was under the yoke of him whom Jesus, in the Gospels, calls "the prince of this world" or Satan. Having won man's consent in the garden of Eden, the serpent has kept the world well within his grasp. He keeps man, his accomplice in evil, in "darkness and in the shadow of death."

The Incarnation marks the beginning of the great duel that concludes in the victory of the risen Christ. A new phase of human history begins in which Christ is *Lord*. He possesses all power not only in Heaven but also on earth. He is "far above every Sovereignty, Authority, Power, or Domination" because the Father has "put all things under his feet" (Eph. 1:21-22). The risen Christ is Lord of the cosmos and Lord of history. The full significance of the liturgical acclamation should not be missed: "For the kingdom, the power and the glory are yours now and for ever."

The power of evil sometimes seduces us to think the contrary. Christians, especially in times of trial, often seem to doubt not only the power of Christ but also His very existence. The world, however, is really His and He holds the key to the human heart. Satan's is but a false power. Nothing can resist the grace of Christ. He permits evil to weave its web so as to confound evil. When God says "enough," evil is finished. One of the most important teachings of the book of Revelation is the absolute supremacy of Christ over demonic powers. Every individual, group, nation—the entire human race—is under the influence of His grace, which does what it likes. Naturally, it respects man's liberty, but its omnipotence is seen in the achievement of those ends which are set in complete respect for man's free will. St. Thomas Aquinas summarizes this beautifully when he says that "the will of God is always done."[21]

Times of Mercy and Forgiveness

Another fundamental aspect of the final phase of human history is its envelopment in God's mercy. When Christ ascended into Heaven, the Holy Spirit was poured out on the world. This event does not cease with the birth of the Church. It is a perennial Pentecost which lasts to the end of time, when Christ will consign the Kingdom to the Father and God will be all in all.

At the outset of His mission Christ saw the heavens open and the Spirit descend on Him. So too, the heavens open and God pours out His infinite love in the gift of the Holy Spirit to the Church at the outset of her mission. The same outpouring continues in the Church's sacraments and will never cease because God's love for the world is irrevocable. This must always be borne in mind, especially when we are confronted by the apocalyptic scenarios so often proclaimed by many self-authenticated private revelations about the end of time. Many such visions speak of tremendous punishments, another worldwide flood, fire, or even atomic destruction. It cannot be denied that God permits those punishments which man inflicts on himself by his own hands, for example, in war and in those situations brought about by moral disorders. Natural disasters, too, can be seen in this light.

We should not, however, forget that we live in the era of mercy and forgiveness, where punishments purify man and bring him to God. In His wisdom, God permits man to taste the bitter chalice of evil so that he might be freed from the deceit of seduction and return to his heavenly Father Who loves him. Some Christians

---

[21] See St. Thomas Aquinas, *Summa theologica*, I, q. 19, art. 6.

lose sight of the fact that the real flood of the present era is that of God's love. God envelops the whole world with the waters of His life-giving love. The Word Incarnate, God and man, is in Heaven. He is our friend and brother who continually intercedes for us and for the world. How can we entertain terrifying prospects about the future of the world when that same world is loved by an infinite, perennial, faithful love and when Christ Himself rules with an iron scepter?

The Existence of Evil

The Christian must always be conscious of a fundamental datum of faith: the world has been redeemed at a high price and divine mercy shines on it. This necessarily optimistic view of faith is not blind to the existence of evil. The New Testament concurs in the affirmation that the world has been torn away from the Evil One. By divine permission Satan, nevertheless, retains the capacity to operate and destroy. The Kingdom of Christ is not yet realized in the "power and great glory" which will accompany Christ's second coming (Luke 21:27). In his famous letter to the Thessalonians, where he alludes to the mystery of evil, Paul affirms that the forces of evil continue to attack the kingdom. While these have been conquered by the Passover of Christ, they have not ceased to attack, seduce, and persecute the faithful. The New Testament images of Satan's actions are not comforting. Peter portrays him as a raging lion constantly searching out his prey to devour it (1 Pet. 5:8). John compares him to the great red dragon who, thrown down from the heavens, rages against the woman, the Son born to her, and His descendants or those who keep the commandments of God and witness to Jesus Christ (Rev. 12:1–17). We live, therefore, in a time of expectation, vigilance, and struggle.

The Wrath of God

Christians have to avoid two opposing attitudes, both of which are incompatible with the Christian faith. The first fails to appreciate the pervasive and perverse power which has been subdued by Christ and from which the world has been liberated. In His wisdom, God permits it to act in the world until the end of history when it will be cast down into the "lake of fire and sulphur" (Rev. 20:10). Denial of the action of Satan, in this final phase of history which we are living, is a radical departure from the vision of the *Catechism of the Catholic Church* and the Magisterium of the Church.

The other attitude, equally erroneous, exalts the power and activity of Satan to such a degree that it would seem that the world is not subject to the dominion of Christ and that the Christian cannot overcome it with the witness of faith. In this respect, it must be recalled that even the darkest descriptions contained in the Bible, especially those concerned with the struggles at the end of time, conclude with the victory of Christ and His faithful. The Christian should not underestimate the trials, struggles, seductions, and temptations marking his journey and that of the Church in this life. However, he knows that Christ is victorious and that the future is in His hands.

The Glorious Coming of Christ

The final phase of human history, which we are living, will come to an end with the coming of Christ in glory. This datum of faith is of fundamental importance. It is not accidental that the Bible ends by affirming with Christ that His coming is imminent. "The one who guarantees these revelations repeats his promise: I shall indeed be with you soon. Amen; come, Lord Jesus" (Rev. 22:20). As our lives end in particular judgment, so too will man's journey end with the coming of Christ, the judge, who will judge the living and the dead as the *Credo* states. The history of the world will conclude with the arrival of Christ.

It is worth mentioning that there is no shortage of self-proclaimed private revelations positing an intermediate coming of Christ. These are usually connected with millenarianism. The Christian faith, however, envisages only two comings: the first in the humility of the flesh, the second with the power and glory reserved for the end of the world. An intermediate coming of Christ, inaugurating a period of peace and prosperity before His final coming, is a departure from the Christian faith as authoritatively presented in the *Catechism of the Catholic Church* (673–677). In accordance with the New Testament, it must be emphasized that the second coming of Christ is continually pending, even if is not for us to "know times or dates that the Father has decided by his own authority" (Acts 1:7). The Christian knows that the future is in the hands of God and consequently is unable to make any prognostications about it. As with human history, so too with our lives: the future does not belong to us. The admonition of Christ on this matter is peremptory: "stand ready because the Son of Man is coming at an hour you do not expect" (Matt. 24:44). St. Paul, in several texts, stresses that it is impossible to predict the moment chosen by the Lord. In His day, as in ours, self-proclaimed private revelations pretended to contain the day and the hour of the Lord's coming. The Apostle exhorts:

> You will not be expecting us to write anything to you, brothers, about "times and seasons," since you know very well that the Day of the Lord is going to come like a thief in the night. It is when people are saying "How quiet and peaceful it is" that the worst suddenly happens, as suddenly as labor pains come on a pregnant woman; and there will be no way for anybody to evade it. (1 Thess. 5:1–3)

These words reveal the trials of the end times, but they also emphasize the unexpected and unknown character of the moment of the Lord's coming.

The Christian, therefore, hesitates when presented with private revelations which put a specific date on the coming of Christ in glory at the end of the world. He is not anxious to deny absolutely the possibility that God may reveal the future to His saints and to especially chosen souls. The prophecy of Fatima about events of this century has been deemed credible by the Church. The revelation of future events, always part of the Church's history, is one thing. The revelation of the day of the Lord which Christ has kept from man is quite another:

> If anyone says to you then, "Look, here is the Christ" or, "Look, he is there," do not believe it; for false Christs and false prophets will arise and produce signs and portents to deceive the elect, if that were possible.... But as for that day or hour, nobody knows it, neither the angels of heaven, nor the Son: no one but the Father. (Mark 13:21–22, 32)

This does not imply that the Christian should not discern the signs of the times and reflect upon them. The only answer that we can give to the question of whether we have arrived at the end of time is that of Paul VI: "We shall never know!"

Recognition of Israel

Every page of the New Testament displays intense reflection on Christ's second coming. It is a fresco describing the Church's pilgrim journey through this final phase of history and the trials confronting her at the conclusive moment of this last period when the powers of evil will unleash their last and most intense assault. We can be grateful to Paul for his deeply significant theological meditation by which, in a certain sense, we can glean from history those signs indicating that the second coming is about to happen. According to the Apostle, the coming of the Messiah in glory is suspended at every moment of history until His recognition by all Israel.

Chapter eleven of the Epistle to the Romans is a profound reflection on the role of Israel in salvation history. According to St. Paul, the chosen people of Israel have a role to play precisely in relation to the end of time: "Since their rejection meant the reconciliation of the world, do you know what their admission will mean? Nothing less than a resurrection from the dead!" (Rom. 11:15.) Paul regrets that part of the chosen people hardened in their unbelief toward Jesus. In God's merciful design, however, their rejection obtained the grace of redemption. If their rejection results in the salvation of the world, what significance can their acceptance have, other than the admission of the world to the glory of the risen Christ? In other words, the recognition of Jesus as Messiah and Lord by the Jewish people will mean that human history has reached its conclusion.

This conviction of faith was already well established in the first Christian community. Peter, even before Paul, alludes to it in his preaching to the Jews of Jerusalem after Pentecost:

> Now you must repent and turn to God, so that your sins may be wiped out, and so that the Lord may send the time of comfort. Then he will send you the Christ he has predestined, that is Jesus, whom heaven must keep till the universal restoration comes which God proclaimed, speaking through his holy prophets. (Acts 3:19-21)

What is the origin of the Apostolic Church's conviction of faith which closely links the second coming of Christ with the conversion of all of Israel? The Gospels well reflect this idea when Jesus, pondering on the rejection of Jerusalem, foretells the destruction of the Temple which, in turn, is a prophetic sign of the sufferings of the end of time:

> Jerusalem, Jerusalem, you that kill the prophets and stone those who are sent to you! How often have I longed to gather your children, as a hen gathers her chicks under her wings, and you refused! So be it! Your house will be left to you desolate, for, I promise, you shall not see me any more until you say: Blessings on him who comes in the name of the Lord! (Matt. 23:37–39)

We can conclude that, in the Catholic sense of the end of time, the coming of Christ in glory is closely linked to His acceptance by the chosen people of Israel. Does this imply that there will be no end of the world until after the conversion of the Jews? On this point the *Catechism of the Catholic Church* states: "The 'full inclusion' of the Jews in the Messiah's salvation, in the wake of 'the full number of the Gentiles,' will enable the People of God to achieve 'the measure of the stature of the fullness of Christ,' in which 'God may be all in all'" (674). This means that it is reasonable to suppose that the end of time and Christ's coming as judge will not happen until after His acceptance by all of Israel. Mary's fiat made possible His first coming in the humility of the flesh. Israel's acceptance will make possible His second coming in power and glory.

The End Times

We have called the phase of human history we are living in the "end times." This phrase embraces the period between the Ascension and the Parousia. We do not know the duration of this definitive phase of history in which man is offered the grace of salvation. However, we should remember one thing: the preceding period of expectation and waiting, beginning with the Fall and the expulsion of Adam and Eve from Paradise, was a very long period and extended over hundreds of thousands of years. God is not as impatient as we

> with the Lord, "a day" can mean a thousand years, and a thousand years is like a day. The Lord is not being slow to carry out his promises, as anybody else might be called slow; but he is being patient with you all, wanting nobody to be lost and everybody to be brought to change his ways. The Day of the Lord will come like a thief, and then with a roar the sky will vanish, the elements will catch fire and fall apart, the earth and all that it contains will be burned up. (2 Pet. 3:8-10)

It is certain that the world will come to an end. Science assures us that, at least, our planet will end. We do not know when. But waiting and watching can last for an indeterminate period of time. God's measures are not ours. The waiting period for the first coming was very long. How can we exclude the possibility that the waiting period for the second coming will not be longer?

Divine revelation, which does not mention any specific time or day, does not subordinate the second coming to the conversion of Israel. Rather it places it in a precise context.

Christ describes frightening scenes. The last days preceding the second coming will be marked by a final trial which will shake the faith of many believers. Jesus asks: "But when the Son of Man comes, will he find any faith on earth?" (Luke 18:8). This is a mysterious phrase, but its immediate meaning cannot be escaped. Only a "little flock" will persevere in the faith until the end, awaiting the Lord's coming. The greater part of mankind, including many believers, will have lost the faith.

In another context Jesus adds to the eclipse of faith a cooling of charity. Indeed, it is not possible to lose one without losing the other. Thus, he describes the "trials" of the end times: "Many false prophets will arise; they will deceive many, and with the increase of lawlessness, love in most men will grow cold; but the man who stands firm to the end will be saved" (Matt. 24:11–13). Jesus situates the end of the world in the context of great apostasy from the faith. The rejection of Christianity by many who had adhered to it will take place in a world where the Gospel of the Kingdom has been proclaimed to the ends of the earth (cf. Matt. 24:14). The coming of Christ as judge will take place in a context of betrayal.

The Church's Ultimate Trial

In the wake of Christ, the apostles, especially John and Paul, further characterize the last and most serious trial to be confronted by the Church before meeting her Lord. The most disconcerting account is that of Paul in his second letter to the Thessalonians:

> To turn now, brothers, to the coming of our Lord Jesus Christ and how we shall all be gathered around him: please do not get excited too soon or alarmed by any prediction or rumor or any letter claiming to come from us, implying that the Day of the Lord has already arrived. Never let anyone deceive you in this way. It cannot happen until the Great Revolt has taken place and the Rebel, the Lost One, has appeared. This is the Enemy, the one who claims to be so much greater than all that men call "god," so much greater than anything that is worshiped, that he enthrones himself in God's sanctuary and claims that he is God. Surely you

remember me telling you about this when I was with you? And you know, too, what is still holding him back from appearing before his appointed time. Rebellion is at its work already, but in secret, and the one who is holding it back has first to be removed before the Rebel appears openly. The Lord will kill him with the breath of his mouth and will annihilate him with his glorious appearance at his coming. But when the Rebel comes, Satan will set to work: there will be all kinds of miracles and a deceptive show of signs and portents, and everything evil that can deceive those who are bound for destruction because they would not grasp the love of the truth which could have saved them. (2 Thess. 2:1–12)

According to Paul, the great apostasy of the end times will be caused by someone who comes as the supreme enemy of God and who operates as the instrument of Satan whose superhuman power he has received, in a way like the spirit of Christ which is communicated to Christians. He is sealed with three names. He is the "man of impiety," the "son of perdition," that is, the man destined for his own destruction, and "the adversary of God." He is clearly a personal being who will manifest himself in the end times, while Satan, whose instrument he is, even now operates in "secret," exercising a persecutory and seductive power against believers—as is affirmed by John in Revelation when he evokes the beast similar to a panther and the beast similar to a lamb (cf. Rev. 13:1–18).

Paul attributes the delay of the Parousia to something or someone impeding the manifestation of the Antichrist, who must precede the Parousia. Notwithstanding many theories advanced about this, we still do not know what it might be. It is important, however, to emphasize that the mystery of iniquity is already at work and through its work, the great apostasy will be brought about. Once the obstacle has been removed, the Antichrist will appear and act openly. At the height of his ascent, Christ the judge will come and destroy him.

We should not think that this scenario is exclusive to the end times when there will be a great "religious impostor" and the coming of the Antichrist in person. In the course of the Church's history the mystery of iniquity has not ceased to deploy its weapons of persecution and seduction. In this regard St. John is very instructive:

> Children, these are the last days; you were told that an Antichrist must come, and now several antichrists have already appeared; we know from this that these are the last days. Those rivals of Christ came out of our own number, but they had never really belonged; if they had belonged, they would have stayed with us; but they left us, to prove that not one of them ever belonged to us.... The man who denies that Jesus is the Christ—he is the liar, he is Antichrist; and he is denying the Father as well as the Son." (1 John 2:18–22)

The entire time span between the first and second coming of Christ will be subjected to seduction and persecution. Every generation will have its "epiphanies" of the mystery of iniquity. The false Christs, the false prophets and the persecutors always accompany the Church on the pilgrim journey. Jesus prophesied that "a servant is not greater than his master. If they persecuted me, they will persecute you too" (John 15:20). Hence, any era can be a background for situations and persons who anticipate the drama of the end times. The book of Revelation can teach us much about this. On the one hand, in describing the final great trial, it looks to the future, while on the other, it meditates on past events experienced by the Christian community—events such as the persecutions of Nero and Domitian which are portrayed as prophecies of the final drama. The same perspective is to be found in the Gospels. Jesus certainly describes the end times in His eschatological discourse. He sees the imminent destruction of Jerusalem as an anticipatory prophecy of the suffering of the end times.

What is the significance of all these signs? They invite every Christian generation to vigilance and prayer. Only the last generation will see the days of the Antichrist and the time of the supreme trial. All other generations, however, will equally have seen the mystery of iniquity in its various manifestations. Christians do not belong to the world and every generation must bear the hatred of the world. At any stage in the Church's history Satan, Antichrist, may have tried to seduce and destroy her. In a certain sense, every generation has its own antichrists who can be regarded as persecutors anticipating the final struggle when the great man of iniquity will manifest himself.

The Supreme Deception

Up to this point we have closely followed the biblical texts which the Church, in the course of history, has reflected on. Now we come to examine the interpretation of these texts provided by the *Catechism of the Catholic Church*, which affords some very interesting points. The key terms used by the New Testament to describe satanic action against the Church during the course of her history, especially in the end times, are "persecution" and "seduction." The two beasts of Revelation correspond to these two activities of the red dragon. The *Catechism of the Catholic Church* makes an important contribution to the understanding of these terms.

In what does this seduction, whose greatest expression is the appearance of the Antichrist, consist? We know that the New Testament refers to false prophets who present deception as truth and who especially deny that Jesus is the Christ, the Son of God (1 John 2:22). The *Catechism of the Catholic Church* employs an original terminology and speaks of "a religious deception offering men an apparent solution to their problems at the price of apostasy from the truth. The supreme religious deception is that of the Antichrist, a pseudo-messianism by which man glorifies himself in place of God and of His Messiah come in the flesh" (675).

Benson's novel amply develops the meaning of this text—not an insignificant achievement for the author. Here we are confronted with a radical rejection not only of the Church and of Christ, but also of God himself. Man takes the place of God and becomes the arbiter of His own life, of good and evil, and of destiny. Man seeks to build a godless world and resolve the fundamental questions of existence in sole reference to his own capacities. The Antichrist incarnates this spirit and the project of constructing a world which, having eliminated God, deifies and absolutizes itself.

What are the biblical roots of this interpretation of the final seduction to which the Church will be subjected? St. Paul describes the end times as those in which the world will think that it has suc-ceeded in establishing peace and security (1 Thess. 5:3) through the man of iniquity who, in virtue of his success obtained by the power of Satan, will take his place in the temple of God (2 Thess. 2:4).

In the background, however, there is a very clear parallel be-tween the trials suffered by Christ and those which the Church must necessarily undergo during the course of her history, especially at the end times. From the beginning, the Gospels tell us, Satan tries to guide Christ into a false messianism based on the power to turn stones to bread, to enthrall the multitudes with miracles,

and finally to dominate the world by political means. This temptation, which Christ rejected by His acceptance of the Cross, will
always accompany the Church on her pilgrim journey and will be
especially present to her in the end times.

How many will resist the spell of secularized messianism which
Pius XI declared "intrinsically perverse"? It cannot be denied that
the religious deception described in the *Catechism of the Catholic
Church* is a distinctive characteristic of our own times. Recent centuries have seen the rise of humanitarian religion, man's attempt
to achieve a salvation by political forms of secularized messianism.
The illusion of creating an earthly paradise, devoid of God, by
man's own capacity is very tenacious. When one form of political messianism fades, other more subtle forms emerge to delude
man into believing that he can become lord of the world and of
life. For the first time in the history of man, atheism has become
a mass phenomenon. Man dreams of shaping the future by his
own resources, without regard for God or the moral law. Many
abandon the faith and the Christian understanding of life, deluded
that the world solves all the problems of existence.

Are these really the characteristics of the end times? It is impossible to say. Even if our own times may well be an important
manifestation of the Antichrist's seduction, how can we be certain that we are really facing the great religious deception of the
Antichrist? In the end, it is not so important for us to know the
hour of the Son of Man. No one can be certain of its arrival until it appears "like lightning striking in the east and flashing far
into the west" (Matt. 24:27). We shall only know with certainty
that the hour has come when we see Him coming on the clouds
and the angels sound the great trumpet that will gather the elect
from the four winds. Before this, it will be necessary to have the
discernment of faith and the strength to bear witness even unto

martyrdom. In the past, many Christians thought that their trials were those of the end times. This was not so. No one can know with certainty that the sufferings experienced by this generation are the final tribulations.

The Church's Passion

The *Catechism of the Catholic Church* sets out some convincing reflections on the other aspect of the Church's final trial—persecution. This has also accompanied the people of God for its entire earthly pilgrimage. Jesus holds out no prospects for a Christianity accommodated to the world. He warns: "Men will seize you and persecute you; they will hand you over to the synagogues and to imprisonment, and bring you before kings and governors because of my name" (Luke 21:12). Martyrdom, in its profound sense of witness to the point of laying down one's life, is part of normal Christian life.

In the last days, however, this possibility will become very real for the entire Church. Theories of millenarianism have spurred the Church to reflect on the ultimate stages of her earthly journey. Rather than the triumphant march of millenarianism, it will be a carrying of the cross ending on Calvary. Thus the Church is called to relive, in herself, the paschal mystery of Christ. The *Catechism of the Catholic Church* is most striking in this respect: "The Church will enter the glory of the kingdom only through this final Passover, when she will follow her Lord in his death and Resurrection" (677).

The *Catechism of the Catholic Church* begins from an incontestable theological presupposition. The Church is a prolongation in history of the mystery of Christ and the members of the mystical Body are called to relive in themselves the life of their Head. The public life of Jesus is marked by preaching, witness, temptation, and persecution. It is the same for the Church on her journey through history. Jesus' life concludes with His entry into the mystery of cruel suffering even unto death on the cross, ignominy, and aban-donment. When everything seemed consummated and when the powers of evil seemed to taste decisive victory, divine omnipotence intervened to destroy the powers of darkness and to raise to the splendor of glory Him whom the world sought to destroy.

The Church in the final stages of her earthly pilgrimage will be called to relive the same Passion of Christ, so as to enter into the glory of the Parousia. Like Christ, she will know the anguish of Gethsemane. She will be betrayed, abandoned by many of her children, mocked, derided, scourged, condemned to death, and crucified. When the world thinks that it has succeeded in erasing her from the face of the earth and begins to sing its victory, at that moment the true Lord of the World will appear on the clouds and bring the Church into the divine glory of the Resurrection.

Contrary to certain forms of millenarianism and triumphalism, "the kingdom will be fulfilled, then, not by a historic triumph of the Church through a progressive ascendancy, but only by God's victory over the final unleashing of evil, which will cause his Bride to come down from heaven" (*Catechism of the Catholic Church*, 677). The world in fact will follow the dragon and the two beasts and adore them:

> The whole world had marveled and followed the beast. They prostrated themselves in front of the dragon because he had given the beast his authority; and they prostrated themselves in front of the beast ... and all people of the world will worship it, that is, everybody whose name has not been written down since the foundation of the world in the book of life of the sacrificial Lamb. (Rev. 13:3-8)

Many "private revelations" literally interpret the kingdom of a thousand years mentioned in Revelation. Some authors, such as

Soloviev and Maria Valtorta, adopt an apocalyptic scheme positing the appearance of the Antichrist before the thousand-year kingdom, at the end of which, they see the final unleashing of the power of evil. This is followed by the Parousia. The Church has never adopted such a view and, as we have amply illustrated, sees the Antichrist in the context of the supreme religious deception which precedes the last days and the coming of Christ in glory.

How do we interpret the thousand-year kingdom so fully described in Revelation?

> I saw an angel come down from Heaven with the key of the Abyss in his hand and an enormous chain. He overpowered the dragon, that primeval serpent which is the devil and Satan, and chained him up for a thousand years.... I saw the souls of all who had been beheaded for having witnessed for Jesus and for having preached God's word, and those who refused to worship the beast ... they came to life, and reigned with Christ for a thousand years. (Rev. 20:1-6)

Literal interpretations of this text have caused not a few writers to err from the perspective of the faith. John has just described the great persecution of the Church, firstly under Nero and subsequently under Domitian. He encourages Christians and reassures them that after the persecution God will grant a period of peace and renewal to the Church. The resurrection of the martyrs must also be seen symbolically as their persistent spiritual presence in the Church's journey to recovery.

From a theological perspective this interpretation is absolutely correct. The Church's pilgrim journey is characterized by times when the dragon rages with seduction and persecution, and also by times when God grants peace and tranquility. This is also true at an individual level. Woe to us were God to allow the Devil to attack us always. This does not imply, however, that temptation has disappeared from our lives. It signifies that the wisdom of God has reduced its intensity and danger. The "mystery of iniquity" continues its attack on the Church to the extent permitted by God, who provides for His pilgrim people, assuring them alternative periods of tribulation and peace.

Undoubtedly at the end of time there will be an unsatiable unleashing of the forces of darkness, such as had never happened before. This is the time of the supreme deception and of the Antichrist, of the final battle and the triumph of God over insurrection and evil:

> When the thousand years are over [that is, after the period of peace which God will give to the Church], Satan will be released from his prison and will come out to deceive all the nations [that is, God will permit him to launch his final attack] in the four quarters of the earth, Gog and Magog, and mobilize them for war. His armies will be as many as the sands of the sea; they will come swarming over the entire country and besiege the camp of the saints, which is the city that God loves. But fire will come down on them from heaven and consume them. Then the devil, who misled them, will be thrown into the lake of fire and sulphur, where the beast and the false prophet are, and their torture will not stop, day or night, for ever and ever. (Rev. 20:7-10)

This famous text, taken with Paul's second letter to the Thessalonians, gives a clear message. When the "supreme deception" appears to have overcome and when the Church's destruction seems imminent and inevitable, when the mystery of iniquity appears in the Antichrist, because he is no longer delayed, when the Church has drunk the last drop from the chalice of the Lord's passion, then the triumph of God over the powers of evil will issue in the form of the last or universal judgment while the Church will come down from Heaven adorned like a bride for her spouse (cf. Rev. 20:11–21:2).

Naturally, we wonder if the time of the persecution and of the great unleashing of evil is being prepared. No certain answer can be given to this question. Every era has experienced the seduction and persecution of the Church by the mystery of iniquity. In some instances it has been particularly intense. At other times the world appears to return to God. The only important thing for every individual and for every generation is to emerge with the palm of victory for, in the final analysis, this is what counts.

The Power of Hell Will Not Prevail

What we do not know about the end of time, since God has not revealed it to us, and what we have summarized from the biblical texts and the interpretation given to them by the Church, especially in The *Catechism of the Catholic Church*, is a bimillenarian reflection. No private revelation can modify or replace what is already the established doctrine of the Magisterium. Neither can particular details deriving from private revelations be accorded the same weight or authority as official teaching. It is sufficient for the informed Christian, when confronted with such matters, to know that trusting in other sources can be misleading.

There has been no shortage of private revelations, even of saints such as Hildegard of Bingen (1098–1179) and St. Bridget of Sweden (1303–1373). While the Church recognizes the sanctity of persons, she does not pronounce anything concerning private revelations, unless they are clearly within the bounds of right doctrine. We can take into account what such revelations say, provided they remain within the framework of the faith. Prudent discernment, however, is necessary in this task. Some presumed revelations made by Jesus and Our Lady current in Catholic circles can be perplexing. Among simple people, they feed the legend of the Antichrist who is said to occupy the chair of Peter or those in its immediate vicinity. Indeed, the theme of the corruption of the Church has been so overworked that it could be asked whether such so-called revelation, produced in Catholic circles, does not echo the fond themes of the sects of every era.

There is no doubt that the Bible alludes to loss of faith and charity during the period preceding the end of the world. Many of the followers of the Antichrist will have betrayed the Church. Neither persecution nor seduction, however, can corrode the Chair of Peter and the apostolic college united with it—even if some of its individual members should defect. Christ's promise that "the gates of hell shall not prevail against it" remains valid until the end of history.

Have We Reached the End of Time?

After this schematic presentation of the Catholic doctrine of the end of the world, the question, already present in minds of many as the millennium approaches, can be asked—have the end times come? In this context one aspect of Catholic doctrine must always be emphasized: "The glorious Messiah's coming is suspended at every moment of history until his recognition by 'all Israel'" (*Catechism of the Catholic Church*, 674). We cannot speak of the end of the world until Christ has been recognized by the Jewish people.

Certainly, it will be a fundamental task for every generation to unmask the religious deception ceaselessly woven by the mystery of iniquity. Every era, in the end, experiences, albeit with lesser intensity, the drama of the end of the world. Our times have been marked by great tribulations and have experienced great "religious deception." The real problem is to discover how to emerge strengthened and victorious from these tribulations. The Magisterium, which guides the bark of Peter through the vagaries of time, invites us to look to the future with hope. A favorite theme of the Holy Father[22] sees the Church still only at the beginning of the evangelization of the world. Far from embracing any gloomy outlook, the Pope emphasizes the joyous celebration of the Jubilee, the two thousandth anniversary of the birth of Jesus, as an immediate goal for the Church. The People of God are invited to move toward the future in a penitential spirit, in faith and gratitude.

It is impossible to reconcile disaster and tribulation with such an outlook. When the time of the great deception and tribulation comes, God will not fail to grant the light of discernment to him whom He has placed at the head of the Church.

---

[22] The author is referring to Pope St. John Paul II. —Ed.

About the Author

Fr. Livio Fanzaga was born in Dalmine, in Bergamo, Italy, in 1940. He joined the Piarists, earning a doctorate in theology at the Gregoriana in Rome and a doctorate in philosophy at the Catholic University of Milan. He was assigned to parochial ministry in the parish of St. Joseph Calasanz in Milan. In 1987, he took over responsibility for Radio Maria, then a small parochial radio station, which has since grown into a major Catholic network of international proportions. Fr. Fanzaga is the author of several books.

Sophia Institute

Sophia Institute is a nonprofit institution that seeks to nurture the spiritual, moral, and cultural life of souls and to spread the gospel of Christ in conformity with the authentic teachings of the Roman Catholic Church.

Sophia Institute Press fulfills this mission by offering translations, reprints, and new publications that afford readers a rich source of the enduring wisdom of mankind.

Sophia Institute also operates the popular online resource CatholicExchange.com. *Catholic Exchange* provides world news from a Catholic perspective as well as daily devotionals and articles that will help readers to grow in holiness and live a life consistent with the teachings of the Church.

In 2013, Sophia Institute launched Sophia Institute for Teachers to renew and rebuild Catholic culture through service to Catholic education. With the goal of nurturing the spiritual, moral, and cultural life of souls, and an abiding respect for the role and work of teachers, we strive to provide materials and programs that are at once enlightening to the mind and ennobling to the heart; faithful and complete, as well as useful and practical.

Sophia Institute gratefully recognizes the Solidarity Association for preserving and encouraging the growth of our apostolate over the course of many years. Without their generous and timely support, this book would not be in your hands.

www.SophiaInstitute.com
www.CatholicExchange.com
www.SophiaInstituteforTeachers.org

Sophia Institute Press is a registered trademark of Sophia Institute. Sophia Institute is a tax-exempt institution as defined by the Internal Revenue Code, Section 501(c)(3). Tax ID 22-2548708.